Contents

Dedication	VI
1. Chapter 1	1
2. Chapter 2	7
3. Chapter 3	13
4. Chapter 4	27
5. Chapter 5	33
6. Chapter 6	36
7. Chapter 7	44
8. Chapter 8	49
9. Chapter 9	52
10. Chapter 10	56
11. Chapter 11	60
12. Chapter 12	66
13. Chapter 13	74

14.	Chapter 14	82
15.	Chapter 15	96
16.	Chapter 16	101
17.	Chapter 17	105
18.	Chapter 18	114
19.	Chapter 19	122
20.	Chapter 20	126
21.	Chapter 21	133
22.	Chapter 22	139
23.	Chapter 23	141
24.	Chapter 24	146
25.	Chapter 25	150
26.	Chapter 26	153
27.	Chapter 27	155
28.	Chapter 28	158
29.	Chapter 29	166
30.	Chapter 30	180
31.	Chapter 31	184
32.	Chapter 32	186
33.	Chapter 33	188
34.	Chapter 34	194

COLORING LIFE

VIKKI ALEXANDER

KDP Paperback ISBN: 979-8714052491
Paperback ISBN: 978-1990724237
Ebook ISBN: 978-1-990724-24-4

Cover design by MIBLart

35. Chapter 35	200
36. Chapter 36	209
37. Chapter 37	216
38. Chapter 38	226
39. Chapter 39	233
40. Chapter 40	245
41. Chapter 41	254
42. Chapter 42	257
43. Chapter 43	264
44. Chapter 44	270
45. Chapter 45	272
Acknowledgments	275
About Author	278
Also By	279

To R, P, & G. Thank you for all your love, patience, and encouragement. I could not have done this without you.
"Here's to strong women. May we know them. May we be them. May we raise them." – Unknown

Chapter 1

I GUESS BY NOW I'm considered middle-aged. Not that I feel like it, but the other day, I walked past a mirror and got startled when I saw my mother in my house, realizing a second later, it was me. Years ago, I remember my mom saying, "I still feel as if I'm twenty, and I don't know who that stranger is looking back at me." Now, I understand what she meant.

Not long ago, everyone knew me as Julie Brennan. I was a reliable friend, an average "C" student, and an utterly confused teenager. Today, I am Julianne Brennan Russo—mother of two and wife of Andrew Russo. I am a neighbor, a sister, a friend, and a mother, but there is much more to me than what people see.

I live in a world where everyone drives minivans, BMWs, and Audis. From the outside, my life appears normal—almost perfect, in fact. The women around me play tennis and golf; their kids take piano lessons. It is all part of the world I longed to live in as a child, but I don't belong here. I'm a fraud.

That last thought is how I ended up pacing the worn-out, powder blue carpet in Dr. De Salmo's waiting room. My life has been crumbling around me for years, no matter how much I have been scrambling to save it. I am losing both my family and my sanity.

"I can do this," I assured myself as I plopped down on the worn-out, cracked brown leather sofa. I grimaced as a sharp, torn edge scratched the back of my bare leg. Rubbing the now red spot, I wondered what the difference was between a psychologist and a psychiatrist. Can she give me drugs? Maybe she will put me on Prozac, Zoloft, Lexapro, or Xanax.

I don't trust anyone, not even myself. My experience with the human race has not fostered a sense of security. Instead, I have come to believe if I trust someone, I give them the power to hurt me, and I have been hurt enough. I have learned through the years: people often show a different persona publicly than privately. Most of us hide behind a façade. Some try to hide their vulnerabilities, while others are trying to advance an agenda. I may be jaded but rarely have I met someone who was able to change my opinion. I hide, but there is a very good reason for that.

I was vacillating between self-hate and self-pity when I heard a door open. "Are you Julianne?" I looked up to see an ordinary-looking woman. She had short dark hair and was about five foot six and no more than one hundred and thirty pounds, with her neatly manicured hand extended my way. She wasn't as intimidating as I thought she would be. But then, I'm not sure what I expected.

"Yes, I am." I reached out my hand to shake hers. "You must be Dr. De Salmo."

"You may call me Laura. Please, come on in."

I walked into her small office and settled into the softness of one of the oversized floral chairs tucked into the corner.

"Julianne, what brings you here today?"

"How much time do we have? It's a long story." I laughed nervously.

"Today we have 45 minutes, so let's start with the basics; why did you call me?"

I let out a long sigh, sat up straight, and started. "I don't recognize myself anymore. I used to be so sure that my life was going to work out the way I had planned, and for a while it did, but now I'm losing everything."

"Can you be a little more clear about what you mean?"

"The people in my town think I am one of them. They look at me through their designer sunglasses, asking what time I'm going to yoga. I honestly believed that if I mimicked them long enough, I could be one of them. I could be Julianne instead of plain old Julie."

"What's wrong with being Julie? Is she different from Julianne?"

As I bit the inside of my cheek, I murmured, "Everyone sees Julianne as strong and independent. She wears Lulu Lemon, is a class Mom, and goes to book clubs. She has a successful husband, gorgeous children, and wants for nothing.

"The other day while in yoga, my chest ached as if it was caving in, and I couldn't catch my breath. My anxiety was scratching at my insides trying to break out, kind of like in the movie Alien. Do you know what I mean?"

She didn't answer.

"Anyway, in the middle of class, I peeked out of the corner of my eyes, checking to see if anyone was watching me, but the other women were focused on their intentions. None of them looked to have a care in the world. I managed to bring myself back to center, closed my eyes, and chanted my mantra: Breathe in... Breathe out... *'I'* ... breathe in... breathe out... *'fucking'* ... breathe in... breathe out... *'hate you'.*

"Our yogi ended the class with his familiar Sanskrit prayer: 'Lokah Samastah Sukhino Bhavantu.' May all beings everywhere be happy and free, and may the thoughts, words, and actions of my own life contribute in some way to that happiness and to that freedom for all.

"I rolled up my mat, gave a shallow bow to Ravi, and a quiet, subdued 'Namaste' as I exited the studio, for I knew his words had no meaning for me—I was trapped in a life where I didn't belong.

"Julie is the name I have gone by most of my life, but I didn't want to be her anymore after getting married. She has horrible nightmares, an embarrassing past, and well... I want her to disappear. The me I used to be. She is unlovable and completely screwed up."

"Let's back up a moment. Who did you hate during your yoga practice?"

"Me? My husband? I don't actually know. I hate everything and everyone."

I didn't want to look at Laura for fear that I would recognize the same disapproval I always saw on my mother's face. The look that said I was a nothing—a nobody. Instead, when I raised my eyes to meet Laura's, they were filled with compassion and understanding. She encouraged me to continue with a tender smile on her lips. "Why don't you tell me a little about your husband?"

The tears gathered at the corner of my eyes at the mere thought of Andrew. She handed me a box of tissue.

"He doesn't love me. At least not in the way a husband should love a wife. Not in the way I thought he was going to love me. He lied. He promised he would never hurt me, but that's all he seems to do."

"Julie, how is he hurting you?" I could see the alarm in her eyes; she was thinking physically.

"No, not that way. I almost wish it was. At least I would understand what was going on." What started as a slow trickle of tears became a torrent of sobs. Once the spewing of information was over, I had a slight sense of relief.

"That was a great start. We can work through this together." She made a few notes and closed her notebook.

"So, you don't think I'm crazy?" I was shocked at how easily everything went.

"No, you're not crazy. You've been through a lot, and that's why I'm here. We'll sort everything out.

Change doesn't happen overnight. You will need to be patient."

Being with her made me believe it might be possible. "Okay," I acquiesced with a tentative smirk.

"Same time next week?"

"Yes, same time. Thank you." I left with a smile. I'm going to be all right, I thought.

The appointment had not been what I expected. I thought perhaps I would tell the Doctor a bit about what was happening, and she would give me some advice and possibly a pill. Instead, I sat across from a stranger and told her some of my darkest secrets.

I left Laura's office, wondering how much I would divulge the next time. Did I really want to dig up and dissect my past? I had held everything in for so long; what would happen once I started to let it all out?

Chapter 2

HAVE YOU EVER DRIVEN by a church when a wedding is about to take place and wanted to scream, "Don't do it?" I do. All the time.

To reach my suburban corner of the world, I must drive by a beautiful white church, where every Saturday, there is a wedding taking place. I often watch as the bride stands on the front steps waiting to make her grand entrance. The dress or hair may differ, but each bride has the same euphoric look on her face. She is beaming with happiness and hope for the future, not knowing what is actually on the other side of the door. The person waiting for her is not her prince charming, nor is he the man of her dreams. He is another human being with as many annoying faults as anyone else. Although those faults seem endearing now, someday, they will piss her off to no end. She is about to pledge to be with that man for the rest of her natural-born life. She is planning to grow old with him because for generations, women have been conditioned to find that one great love, marry, and live happily ever after. That wouldn't be a bad thing if there were any possibility we could. No one ever told me that marriage on a typical day is challenging, and nearly impossible on a bad one.

"To know why you feel your marriage is falling apart or 'impossible' as you say, we need to investigate how you felt when your relationship started. How did you and Andrew meet? What events were happening in your life?" I could tell Laura was trying to build an outline of my life.

I never thought I'd relive these moments, but I found myself confiding in Laura as if she were a long-lost friend.

Before I met Andrew, I had been in a long-term relationship, but he was more of a placeholder than a boyfriend. When I awoke the morning of my twenty-fifth birthday, I realized I had to change my life.

Brian was five-foot-ten, with curly auburn hair, light freckles, and hazel eyes speckled with gold. He was the proverbial starving artist. Born with a gift to turn an average piece of paper into a work of art with just a charcoal pencil made him intriguing—poor but intriguing. He showered me with attention and made love to me with a sensuality and ease that it was easy to be content. Still, no matter how sweet he was, he was most definitely not "the one." I knew I had to end our relationship if there was any hope of having the life I always imagined.

Where had the last three years gone? I wondered as I listened to Brian snore with his mouth open. As his pale untrimmed chest rose and fell as I planned out my next move.

Back then, I worked for a small computer sales company in a crappy dead-end job that did not make a difference to anyone other than my employer's bottom line. Roger Morelli, my boss, was the type of man who chewed people up and spits them out without the slightest bit of remorse. He would say or do anything to make more money, convincing himself he was powerful, even if it meant taking advantage of people. He specifically targeted the elderly and underprivileged.

There were three of us who staffed the office. Rhona, an overweight ex-stripper who chain-smoked and screamed out, "fuck you" at least fifty times a day to no one in particular. Harold, an old-time numbers man who spent his hours in the office escaping his overbearing wife. Then there was me—I whiled away the hours inputting orders, matching up invoices, and sending out statements. Our office was a filthy, smoke-filled dump. We spent our days trying to keep Roger in Armani suits and drinking Glenfiddich Scotch. For me, it was all about the paycheck.

Roger's lack of morality didn't end with overcharging customers or his love for the almighty dollar. Daily, I would have to endure some sexual remark or innuendo. 'Hey Jul, come here. I'll show you my jewels if you show me yours.' He thought he was hysterical. As much as I hated my job and him, I had to pay the bills. I couldn't move back home, and there was no one to lend me money; therefore, quitting was not a viable option.

However, that was all about to end. I was young, strong, self-reliant, and proud. At least I was that day. If I were ever going to make a significant change, now would be the time. I walked into Roger's office with my head held high, shoulders back with a sense of authority, and placed my letter of resignation in his hands. He leered at me, exposing his crooked yellow teeth. I did not say one word, not even goodbye. I turned on my heel, walked out with a sway in my hips, and a smile on my face.

I climbed into my beat-up beige Jeep Wrangler and drove back to my apartment. I sat in the driveway, gathering up the nerve to go inside. I was not too fond of confrontation and hated what had to be done next. Taking a deep breath, I walked up the three flights to the small one-bedroom apartment I shared with Brian. I hesitated outside, trying to come up with what to say. I reminded myself that if I didn't take this step now, I would surely wake up someday wondering not where the last three years had gone but the previous thirteen.

I opened the door and found Brian sitting on the green and white plaid sofa we'd bought at a garage sale the year before. The walls were crowded with sketches he had done of me through the years. He turned and gave me a huge smile when he realized I had come in. "Hi, Honey. What are you doing home?"

I walked through our tiny galley kitchen and noticed he washed and put away all the breakfast dishes. The large pile of laundry sitting in the basket for days had magically disappeared. My insides crumbled.

The couch creaked as I plopped down next to him with a heavy sigh, "Hey," I said hesitantly. "I just quit my job."

"Really?" he said, sounding very surprised. "That's great." He took both my hands in his and kissed them. "I hated that you had to work for that jerk. I promise, someday I will make enough money that you won't have to work unless you want to."

I pulled my hands away and turned off the television. "We have to talk. Brian." His face gave away his confusion. "You know I think you are an amazing guy, right? I am so lucky to have you."

"But? I definitely hear a 'but' coming, so just say it, Jul."

"It's not you. It's me." God, that's incredibly cliché, I thought to myself. "I don't know what I want. I'm confused, and you deserve so much more. You deserve to have someone love you completely."

"So, what are you saying? Do you need a break? Do you want me to leave? What exactly do you want?" he was both aggravated and sad.

"I want you to move out." I blurted out quickly, thinking it would be like a band-aid. If I said it fast, maybe it wouldn't hurt as much. His beautiful eyes filled with anguish; I looked away before continuing, "I know the right girl is out there waiting for you. She is unbelievably lucky."

"Don't try to justify this, Jul. The right girl isn't out in the world waiting for me. She is sitting next to me. I knew you were 'the one' the day I met you."

That's when my first tear fell. "I'm such a selfish bitch. I'm sorry." I buried my face in my hands. "God, I am so, so sorry." Within seconds, his hand was on my back, comforting me. He was comforting me.

By the end of the day, he agreed to move out.

Chapter 3

TO THOSE OF US from New Jersey, it is simply known as "The Shore." Bruce Springsteen made it famous with his lyrics of summer love, fast cars, and youth finding their way. That was the backdrop for the first time I thought I was in love.

One summer, Mom booked a two-month-long gig at Harrah's in Atlantic City. She would be the opening act for the parade of second-rate musicians entertaining the tourists that drifted in and out of the casinos.

My sister Sarah and I were thrilled to spend our summer vacation down the shore. It may not have been Long Beach Island, where the rich kids stayed, but we weren't picky. Sarah got a job on the boardwalk hawking water guns and bouncy balls, and I spent hours watching mom rehearse in dark smokey rooms.

Two weeks into the trip, Sarah invited me for ice cream. I jumped at the chance. She never had time for me since she was the 'it' girl at school. As we walked, she told me what we were actually doing. "Don't tell mom, but I have a date for you," she said with a sly smile.

"What? Who? Oh my god, Sarah." I was so excited.

"His name is Ryan. He is nineteen and a lifeguard. Very hot, but you have to promise not to act like a baby." She looked at me sternly. "I like his best friend, but he said I had to bring someone for his buddy."

"I promise I will play it very cool." I adjusted my shorts and refolded my white ankle socks.

We arrived at the ice cream parlor as planned. Sarah was right; he was hot, very hot. He had a deep chocolate tan that made him look exotic. His shoulders were broad, and his chest was hairy. He seemed very mature, in contrast to my inexperienced awkwardness.

Sarah and the other boy took off, leaving Ryan and me to fend for ourselves. He wasn't as inaccessible as I thought he would be. We walked along the beach, jumping over the waves as they crashed on the shore. He showed me his guard stand and put his whistle around my neck, lifting my hair to let the rope settle on my naked neck. My cheeks burned at this innocent, yet flirtatious, gesture. As night began to fall, he held my hand, bringing me in close, engulfing me in his strong arms. We swayed with the breeze as he sang Thunder Road gently in my ear.

Ryan and I spent the summer riding up and down the Garden State Parkway on his motorcycle, exploring various beaches. I would wrap my arms tightly around his waist with the hum of the engine connecting us. When he kissed me, my toes curled. It was the first time I had experienced such an attraction. When summer was over, he called me weekly, telling me how much he missed me, how special I was, and I believed him. I was falling in love.

Months later, my mother left the phone bill on the kitchen table, wanting to know why it was so high. I looked, trying to remember what days and times Ryan and I had spoken, and it didn't match up.

I heard the front door open and ran out to meet Sarah. "Are you calling Ryan?"

"Why would I call him?" her mouth twitched as it often did when caught in a lie.

"Well, someone in this house is calling him other than me, and unless it's Mom, it has to be you."

"Okay. So, we talk on the phone. It's no big deal. You would have never met him if I hadn't introduced the two of you."

"What are you two talking about?"

"Stuff. Leave it alone," she warned me sternly.

"What kind of stuff, Sarah?" She didn't answer. "This isn't funny. Please tell me. I think I love him." I was on the verge of a complete breakdown.

"Oh shit, Jul. I'm sorry." She grabbed me into a hug. "I thought it was just a summer fling. Come on; I have them all the time. They aren't supposed to mean anything, silly girl."

"Did you sleep with him?" I already knew the answer in my gut.

"Yes, but like I said, it was no big deal. You were at Mom's show, and I got drunk, and well, things happen. As I said, he was not a big deal." She laughed, holding her fingers inches apart. I was unsure of what that meant. "Fuck him, Little Sis. We can both do so much better."

So much for summer love.

I cried for months, but that's just the way things were in our house. Nothing was sacred, especially not men... but I digress.

Years later, after Brian and I broke up, I took my meager savings and went in on a beach house rental for July to try to sort out my future plans.

We had six guys and five girls sharing a tiny bungalow on Ocean Avenue in Bradley Beach. The house had three small bedrooms, a pull-out couch, and enough space on the floor for a few air mattresses.

We were able to take possession at two o'clock on July 1st, and by four, everyone stripped themselves of 'real world' clothes and wore next to nothing. Beer bongs were chugged, cigarettes smoked, and the occasional joint was passed. It was mayhem. It was the Jersey shore.

I didn't waste time vying for the best bed; I didn't care where I slept. As everyone yelled over each other, I grabbed my green duffle bag and headed to the bathroom. I dug around looking for my favorite floral bikini and slipped it on. Always hypercritical of myself, I took a glance in the mirror. To my surprise, I didn't look too bad. I grabbed a Bud Light from the stocked refrigerator and cracked open the icy can. A small amount of froth bubbled out, which I slurped up. Once I had my sand chair and my copy of *A Confederacy of Dunces*, I headed for the beach.

I chose a small patch of unclaimed sand away from the crowds. The only thing I needed to make the day perfect was a slice of boardwalk pizza and maybe cheese fries.

I had just begun to ease into my happy place when a male voice saying, "Hi," interrupted my peace. I didn't open my eyes immediately. Silently, I debated if I should pretend to be asleep and hope the person the voice belonged to would go away or if I should acknowledge him. He continued to speak, leaving me no choice.

"I'm Andrew. Hey, are you asleep?"

I opened my eyes, holding my hand up to block the sun's glare. I had no idea who he was, but obviously, he knew me.

"You're in on the house, right?" he questioned, even though he already knew the answer.

A muffled "Yes" came out of my mouth, and he made himself at home next to me.

I raised my chair from its semi-horizontal position, put on my cheap drugstore sunglasses, and turned to my new housemate. Much to my surprise, he too, had a copy of *A Confederacy* on top of his towel.

"So, what chapter are you on?" I pointed with my chin in the direction of the book.

"He just got kicked out of the department store."

"Oh, yeah. I'm a couple ahead of you."

"Is this book supposed to be funny, or is it just me?"

"I'm not sure, but I keep laughing out loud." I giggled.

That started an easy exchange of other literary works we had read and movies we favored. We sat laughing over the dialog in *Murder by Death* and *Young Frankenstein*. We were both able to quote entire passages from *The Godfather*.

We were so lost in conversation that we didn't notice the sun was starting to glip down over the horizon until the evening chill had worked its way through my body. I wrapped myself in my towel, and he carried my chair as we walked back to the house together.

Our housemates were trashed when we returned, so we grabbed some clothes and headed to the food vendors to satisfy my craving for a couple of slices with a side of cheese fries. Our legs dangled over the boardwalk's edge while we ate and slurped our colas. Our legs would touch from time to time, and I could feel myself smiling.

Our conversation never waned. We jumped from music to education to politics and even religion. We never had that awkward silence I had experienced with so many before.

We sat in our world while everyone else took off for the bars. Andrew was different from the men I had previously let into my life. Most were pretty basic and easy to figure out. Their four basic primordial needs drive them: eat, sleep, drink, and fuck—not necessarily in that order. These are their weaknesses. From what I could tell, that wasn't Andrew. He was quiet, intelligent, and with a dry sense of humor. He didn't need to prove himself with outlandish behavior or catcalling girls. His silence spoke to a maturity and stability I had never seen before in someone so young. I was surprisingly flattered by his attention. I could sense he was an outsider, like me.

Once at the house, our conversation led us into the early hours of the morning. Sometime around three o'clock, he leaned over to kiss me. It was a sweet and tender kiss, not passionate or desperate. The moment was interrupted when our housemates stumbled in, passing out where they fell.

We smiled at each other. He put his arm around me. I placed my head on his shoulder, and that was how we fell asleep. He didn't touch me or try to take advantage of me. When I awoke several hours later, he was still holding me.

"Have you been up the whole time?" I lilted.

"Yes, I was watching you sleep." It was perhaps the sweetest thing I had ever heard. Because of that one simple statement, I knew he was different. I was different when I was around him. Andrew wasn't only into my looks, but into my brain. I had never had that before. He was the last thing I thought I would find that summer, but I was sure glad I did.

The remainder of the weekend continued much the same way. We read our matching books and compared perspectives while dragging off the same cigarette. We drank lots of beer and ate tons of boardwalk food, from hot dogs to ice cream, and he even won me a teddy bear at the shooting arcade. Men had given me many things over the years, but no one had ever won me a stuffed animal. The innocence alone was intoxicating.

As all good things do, our weekend had to end. Andrew was only down for three days. Unlike me, he had a job awaiting him as an accountant for an internationally recognized firm in New York City. Although under thirty, his career was well on its way. We stood beside his car, holding hands, putting off his inevitable departure.

"I really have to go now," he insisted.

"I know," I said, leaning in and pressing my body against his.

"No, really, I have to go."

"Yes, really, I know." I grazed my lips against his neck.

"You are making this impossible."

"That's the point," I whispered.

I kissed him goodbye, and he promised to call later. I stood and watched as his silver Honda Civic pulled out of sight. I didn't leave the house for the remainder of the evening, in case he called. I understood it came off as pathetic, but I couldn't and wouldn't take the chance of fucking this up. I waited all night, but the phone never rang. Nor did it ring the next day or the day after that. Every day, I convinced myself that somehow, I had screwed things up again.

While everyone was at the beach having fun, I sat in the house staring at the silent white phone. Four days had passed since Andrew left, and I hadn't heard a word from him.

"Did he call?" my best friend Danni wanted to know, looking for her daily update.

"No. I don't think I'm gaining a boyfriend, just weight by the day. Dan, I'm on my fourth pint of Chunky Monkey ice cream!"

"Back away from the spoon, Jul. Put it down and throw out the container."

"What the hell am I going to do?" I sobbed in self-pity.

"You don't even know him. Why are you giving him such power? You are too good for that piece of shit. Starting over, remember?"

"Damn, this is not going very well, is it? Okay, well, at least I didn't waste too much time on him. That fucking douche bag, user, idiot, liar, scumbag, asshole." I relished the act of unburdening myself, so much so that I started to crack up when I finished.

"Yeah. he's an asshole, and better you find that out now than after you fall in love."

"Thank you so much for always being there for me. I don't know what I would do without you."

"What the hell are you talking about? You have been there for me ever since we were little girls. You have never let me down, not once. This is the least I could do. Now pull yourself together and go have some fun."

Of course, Danni was right. She spent the next ten minutes bolstering my self-confidence to get me through the rest of the day—dairy, alcohol, and nicotine-free.

That night I went out with the rest of my housemates. Thursday night was one-dollar shots at the local bar. I remember the first five lemon drops, but everything was all a blur after that. I'm unsure how or when I got home, but I was lying on the bathroom floor curled around the toilet when I woke up. Bracing myself to stand, I held onto the sink for balance. The stench of puke was everywhere.

Looking around, I found chunks in my hair and on my clothes; the aroma permeated my nostrils. I stripped and entered the shower. As I washed, there was a loud knock at the door.

"Yo, Jul, telephone. It's lover boy!" said one of my housemates as immaturely as a thirteen-year-old.

Drying off quickly, I ran to the phone with shampoo still oozing out of my hair. "Hello," I said breathlessly. I almost didn't recognize my voice croaking with the toxins of the night before.

"Julie? Is that you?"

"Uh, yeah. Hi, Andrew," I said. I tried to sound nonchalant, but every nerve in my body was tingling.

"I'm sorry I haven't called. I had to go to London for work. I just got in from the airport," he explained. A wave of relief washed over me. He hadn't blown me off after all. "I hope you're not mad. Do you want to meet me in the city for a drink Friday night?"

I hemmed and hawed for a moment, making him wait for my answer. I wasn't able to hold out long. "I'd love to. How about eight o'clock at Penn Station, in front of the departure board?"

"Perfect! It's a date. See you Friday."

There it was. We had a date. A real date!

Heeding one of my mother's few pieces of usable advice, I purchased new white boy-short panties and a matching white lace bra, just in case. I found my skin-tight Levi's faded in all the right spots with a rip at the knee and a small white Henley t-shirt showing off a hint of my tan, toned stomach. I tried my outfit on multiple times, making sure there weren't any stains, and I looked put together without seeming like I was trying too hard.

Friday finally came. I showered and shaved meticulously. I took my time, paying attention to every detail. I checked myself in the mirror at every angle until I was satisfied with my reflection.

Penn Station was more crowded than I had expected. I scanned the crowds of commuters and travelers with suitcases searching for his familiar face when our eyes locked. He wore a blue polo, tan chinos, and a pair of brown docksiders with leather laces.

"I was starting to think you might not show," he called to me as we closed the distance between us.

"I would never stand you up." I could not hide my smile.

He took my hand, kissed me on the cheek, and led me down 8th Avenue to 30th Street. We stopped outside an Irish tavern with a pool table, music, and several television screens. The bar was crowded with an eclectic clientele. With Andrew's above-average height, he promptly caught the bartender's attention to order a pitcher of beer. Then he ushered me to the pool tables.

"Do you play?" His eyes shifted in my direction while pouring each of us a beer.

"A little," I said with enough confidence and gleam in my eye to throw him off balance. After he racked the balls, I leaned over the table, knowing he was staring at my ass. I took aim at the white cue ball and splintered the pyramid with a loud crack, sinking two stripes with ease. I winked at him with a certain amount of cockiness and went ahead to scratch the next shot.

He laughed at me. "That's what you get for being a smart ass."

"Well, if you weren't staring at my 'smart ass' so much, I might have been able to concentrate." We flirted throughout the night and brushed against each other as we set up the next game. He was leaning against the table, nervously rolling the cue stick between his palms. He was so adorable I couldn't help myself. Rising on my tippy toes, I gave him a peck on the cheek. "I hope you don't mind."

"Not at all. It was nice." He kissed me back, on the lips.

The two of us spent the rest of the evening laughing and talking while picking songs on the jukebox. We bumped each other out of the way so we could be the ones to select the next song. We both reached to put on *Little Guitars* by Van Halen simultaneously. He put the quarters in, and I pressed the combination of letters and numbers. "Hey, we make a darn good team," I whispered, leaning into him.

At the end of the evening, he walked me to my train. "What are you doing tomorrow?"

"You're not coming back down to the shore?" I was unable to hide the disappointment in my voice.

"No, I can't. I have to help my brother move in the morning, but I'll be done by noon if you're going to be around."

"Okay, maybe I'll wait for you." I gave him a sly smile.

He raised an eyebrow. "Maybe?"

"Definitely, but only if you promise we can go on the roller coaster."

"If you buy the popcorn."

Damn, I was falling fast.

That's when he leaned down. His full lips landed gently on mine. His fingers were stroking the nape of my neck. I pulled away, knowing how easily I could be coerced to go home with him. As I walked away, I wondered if he was still looking.

The next day, we rode all the rides on the boardwalk. He held my hand and tickled my palm with his thumb. I couldn't remember ever smiling so much or meeting someone who had me at ease right from the beginning. I rested my head on his shoulder, feeling like we had been together forever.

The remainder of the summer was more fun than I had ever had. He brought me to my first Yankee game. Our seats were halfway up the stadium, alongside the third-base line. I sat in awe of the panoramic view. I could see everything, the pitchers warming up in the bullpen, the players spitting and smacking each other on the back, psyching themselves up for the challenge ahead.

"Peanuts, peanuts, get your peanuts here," barked a man wearing a pinstripe apron, walking down the stairs in our direction. Andrew put up two fingers, and two bags sailed our way. I ducked; Andrew lifted his hand, deftly pulling them out of midair.

"Here you go, beautiful."

"That was kind of sexy," I said, opening the warm bag. He smiled and blushed a bit.

He taught me how to keep score in our souvenir book. We screamed and high-fived as 'our team' went on to extra innings. When the Yankees won, he picked me up, squeezing me in a bear hug. I had no idea baseball could be so fun?

By the time September rolled around, I had met all his brothers. We went to barbecues, parties, and fishing on his brother Jimmy's boat. They were a rowdy bunch, and I loved each and every one of them.

That was when we began our committed relationship. Next, I needed a new job. Love wasn't going to pay my bills.

During one of the many daily conversations between Danni and me, she had a suggestion. "Jul, what would you think about working for Ray? You know, just until you find something else. His clerk left him without warning, and he is desperate to fill the position. I don't think he can afford to pay you much, but he may be willing to train you."

I couldn't believe what I was hearing. I had been waiting for an opportunity like this. "Absolutely! Give me his number, and I'll call him right now." Raymond's practice specialized in recovering Social Security and disability compensation for the injured and elderly—those who fell through the cracks in the system and had nowhere else to turn—the forgotten ones. I hung up, called Ray, and was offered the job on the spot.

I woke every morning with a purpose. At the end of the day, I was sure I had made a difference. At night, I would lay in my bed and speak with Andrew on the phone for hours. My world was beginning to revolve around when I would see him again.

Chapter 4

SHORTLY AFTER WE BEGAN to date, Andrew invited me over for dinner. As I was walking into his building, another tenant left, so I could go upstairs without him knowing. When I reached the fourth floor, his door was ajar, and I observed him at the stove in his sleeveless t-shirt and jeans that were a tad too short. Some might think he looked nerdy, but I found it incredibly endearing. Flour coated the kitchen, pans and bowls were everywhere, and oil spatter covered the stovetop and cabinets. I spied from the hall until he caught me. "Hey, beautiful, I didn't see you there." He took my hand and led me into the living room, where a tray of assorted cheeses and a glass of Chardonnay awaited my arrival. I sat and sipped as *Vivaldi's Four Seasons* concerto played in the background.

"Happy?" his eyes were aglow with pride.

"I've died and gone to heaven." I feigned passing out and flopped back in my best Scarlet O'Hara imitation.

These memories brought me back to a time when I thought anything and everything was possible.

About six months later, things started to change. At first, I chalked it up **to** my imagination. He started to work later than usual. His calls became less frequent, and our physical relationship was waning.

Just as I thought our relationship was fizzling out, he confessed he loved me. We were lying in his bed eating French bread pizza and watching *Sherlock Holmes* on PBS. I was so caught up in Watson's deduction that I didn't hear him at first. After I didn't respond, he tapped me on the shoulder. "Jul, I love you." I wasn't sure if I had heard him correctly, so I ignored him. He turned off the television. "Aren't you going to say something?"

After ten seconds or so, my voice came out much smaller than intended. "You don't have to say that." I removed my hand from his. "Honestly, I'm not going anywhere." My heart was ready to leap out of my chest. These three words should never be taken lightly. To me, love was everything. Opening that door meant opening my heart and allowing myself to trust him.

"Jul, I understand that you have been through a lot, but please, please, let me in. I promise I'm not going to hurt you. Now or ever." Tears flowed from my eyes, wanting so desperately to believe him. So, I did. I let my guard down and gave him everything.

The following year passed quickly. We effortlessly melded into each other's lives. His family warmly welcomed me. Even his dad, who is a douche with a capital "D."

I waited to let him meet Mom and Sarah. Who knew what would happen if I unleashed the Brennan's on him? I was afraid Jackie would try to bed him or offer him a joint or a line of coke. I didn't want to scare him off that early in the game. I held out as long as I could.

Over dinner one night, I wondered in the abstract, "Do you think we will end up getting married? I'm not pressuring you. I'm just curious."

Without missing a beat, he asked, "Would you marry me?"

"Probably," I beamed, and that was the end of the discussion.

Two months later, he showed up at my place, announcing, "Grab your coat. We're going shopping."

"For what?" I was baffled.

"An engagement ring, of course. You do want one, don't you?"

I didn't know what to say. He wanted to marry me, and, God, yes, I wanted to marry him. Secretly, I wished he'd bought a ring on his own but told myself not everything has to be as it is on television or in the movies.

After hours of browsing the cases filled with perfect stones, we settled on a brilliant-cut solitaire diamond set in yellow gold. How was he going to pop the question? I wondered as we walked back to his car.

He put the key in the ignition and handed me the small gold bag. Confused, I held the corded string with two fingers, letting it dangle in the air. "And what would you have me do with this?"

"What do you think?" He seemed confused.

"Don't you want to ask me a question first?" I smiled with the excitement of the moment, waving my finger around.

"I already did, and you said yes. Go ahead and put it on."

My heart sank. "Okay." I took the purple velvet box out of the bag, opened it, and handed the ring to him. "Could you at least put it on my finger?"

"Sure." He placed the ring on the fourth finger of my left hand. "I'm starving. Let's go to the diner and grab some lunch."

As soon as I got home, I picked up the phone to call Sarah.

"Hey, my sister, guess what happened today?" I was unable to hide the excitement in my voice.

"Well, it sounds big. Spill it!" she demanded.

"Yeah, you might say big. As in a big fat one-carat diamond ring!"

"Oh my god. He didn't!"

"Oh yeah, he did, and guess what? I said, yes!"

We both screamed as if we were little girls in our flannel nighties again. When we finished, Sarah said in all seriousness, "Please don't be annoyed with me; this is my job. I have to ask, are you sure? He's nice but a little quiet and, I don't know, dry. Not that there's anything wrong with that." She took a beat and continued, "Somehow, I always pictured you marrying some handsome hippy or running off to an artist's commune, painting your life away singing Kumbaya with a hot, sweaty hunk standing next to you. Sweetie, he seems a little ordinary."

"He's kind, treats me well, loves me, and makes me laugh. There is nothing ordinary about that. You don't understand now, but you'll love him when you get to know him better."

"If he lets me get to know him better," her tone was snotty.

"Don't be that way. He can be a little shy. We Brennan's can be rather intimidating," I reminded her. "God, I am so crazy about him. I can't believe this is happening. Pinch me!" I flopped back on my bed with the phone still to my ear. I held my hand at arm's length, watching the light bounce off the diamond.

"You do know he's not good enough for you, don't you?" I could hear in her voice she was fighting back the tears.

"Stop that! We're supposed to be happy. I understand that you have been through a lot, but Andrew is different. He is good enough for me, maybe too good. Hey, thanks for being my big sister. I love you."

"I wouldn't want anyone else as my little sis. Now that we are done with that, let's get down to business. I am going to be your maid of honor, aren't I?"

Back then, I would have told you he was too good for me, that I was the one getting the better half of the arrangement. He made me believe in myself. He thought I was funny and smart. What a kick that was. My mom always said I was dumb. She convinced me that the only thing I had to give was my body.

I was good for him, too. I taught him to appreciate some things he had always overlooked. We spent many dawns watching the sun crest over the horizon. The sky would awaken in shades of orange and yellow, like paint on a canvas. He was starting to savor life for the first time. All his friends said that I had brought out something in him they had never seen before. We were what I thought every couple should be.

I continued to reminisce in Laura's office, disclosing things I had never wished to discuss with another living soul.

Chapter 5

My new life was unfolding without much effort. I moved in with Andrew and started to plan our wedding. One evening I walked into the bedroom while he was working and asked, "Hey, Honey. Got a second?"

"What is it, Jul?" He was irritated by the interruption.

"Sorry to bother you, but I want to ask you a quick question. Which flowers do you like better? I was thinking of Birds of Paradise, very exotic, but they might be too tall. Perhaps something a little more traditional, like white roses?"

"Do whatever you want. I don't care," he replied with hostility. As I started to walk out of the room, my soul as deflated as an old helium balloon, I heard him call after me, "Honey, I'm sorry. Come here." I walked over, and he pulled me onto his lap, kissing me on the cheek. "I'm sorry. Why don't you figure out what needs to be done right away? When work eases up a bit, I promise I will jump in with both feet. You may even tell me to back off. Okay?"

"Okay," I said, immediately perking up. "Go back to work, nerd boy. I have a wedding to plan. I promise not to bother you again, your Majesty." Before leaving, I turned to him and said, "I will lavish in all the credit when everyone says how amazing it is!" With that, I stuck my tongue out at him.

"Deal." He gave what seemed like a forced smile, but as long he agreed, I didn't care.

The months quickly passed. As our wedding day approached, Andrew was beginning to withdraw. He would leave for work at the crack of dawn and wouldn't return until late in the evening. We stopped making love altogether, which was not my choice. Many nights, I would reach out to stroke him, but he would turn over, claiming to be tired.

"Andrew, there is something I want to talk about," I told him when I woke up one morning. "I don't understand what's going on with you." He rolled his eyes, not wanting to have the discussion. "Hey, don't do that. I'm serious." I was annoyed at his response. "You're hardly ever home anymore, and we never make love. If you've changed your mind, it's okay. We can call it off or push the date back. I swear, I will be okay with whatever you decide." He didn't say anything, but there was no way I wanted to marry someone who didn't want to marry me.

"Just stop. You're ridiculous. I have an impossible deadline to meet at work, that's all. You are reading so much into everything." He gave me a quick peck. "Go back to sleep. I'll see you tonight. I love you."

"I love you too," My words chased him as he walked out the door.

Of course, he was right. It was just those silly insecurities again. I let it drop, convincing myself everything would be better after the wedding.

Chapter 6

IT FEELS LIKE YESTERDAY, but at the same time, it feels like a lifetime ago. It was October fifteenth, and I had just turned twenty-eight. Fall had always been a significant time of year for me, so it was only fitting that I would marry my most treasured person in the world during this season. I woke up with a smile plastered on my face, excited to begin my new life. Outside my window, the leaves had started to turn crimson practically overnight. I had no doubt the day was going to be magical.

I spent that morning with my sister and my three closest friends. We sat around in our underwear, doing each other's makeup and chatting like teenagers. Danni, my best friend, stood in her blue panties, bare-breasted, and announced, "Julie, I'm not ready for you to be married. I say you call the whole thing off," she whimpered.

"No way, lady, I'm getting married! You can move in with us if you want," I assured her.

"Does he realize he's marrying me today, too?" Danni threw my white wedding shoes on and modeled them in the mirror.

"Of course, we're a package! We always have been." I wrapped my arms around her and squeezed tightly.

It wasn't long before Mary broke up the love fest. "Okay, enough of this sappy shit!"

She poured us each a glass of champagne and made the first toast of the day. "Here's to one more hot babe off the market. We'll miss you, but now there are more men for the rest of us. Cheers!"

Next, Kristy chimed in. "Here's to the past. May it never catch up with us."

"I'll drink to that," I said, draining my champagne.

"There's not much you won't drink to, but then who am I to talk?" Danni chugged down her glass and poured us both another.

When we were little girls, we slept over each other's houses and talked about who we would marry, where the weddings would be, and what we would wear. Would we be young or old when we found our soulmates? Had we met them already? Would we last forever? Those questions, for me, were on the cusp of being answered. One of us had made it. One of us had grown up.

The girls dressed first in their dusty rose dresses with a sweetheart neckline. I carefully stepped into my white applique lace dress. After the final button was fastened and the zipper secured, I looked at myself in the full-length mirror. My curves were still in all the right places. My tea-length dress clung enough to be sexy but provided enough coverage not to be obscene. My long, dark hair had yet to have a single gray strand. My dark-brown eyes sparkled as they always did, but they shone brighter than ever that day.

Andrew never kept up with his Catholic upbringing. He was raised with threats of burning in hell if he broke any of the commandments. It was a house of spare the rod and spoil the child. I think he still holds a grudge. I never practiced any formal religion, so getting married in a church didn't ring true to who we are.

I didn't want to be just another pretty bride. It was the most important day of my life. For me, love was at the top, middle, and bottom of my list of reasons to me to marry. Every night, I prayed for someone who would love me for who I am and wouldn't desert me when things got rough. Someone to be my constant. I didn't care if he had money or power. If he was a college graduate or trade school mechanic. All I cared about was that he loved me honestly and truthfully. I understand I'm not the easiest person. It's not that I'm mean or bossy, bitchy or rude—I'm just A LOT. A lot of everything, and for many, it's too much. But not for him. He understood me and wanted to marry me, anyway.

That afternoon I sat alone in a white limousine as guests dribbled into our venue and found their seats. I caught sight of my future husband walking down the path in his black tuxedo and Ray-Ban sunglasses. He was tall and stocky, with thick, jet-black hair. Not handsome in a Tom Selleck kind of way, but there was something about him. As he approached, his face became clear. He had an enormous grin between the dimples that graced his face. 'God, I love him,' I thought to myself.

My heart filled with gratitude, but then my self-doubt and insecurities started creeping in again. They were always waiting to make their entrance. Why did he choose me? Could he love me as much as I loved him? Am I worthy of being this happy?

I had never been at peace in my life, but that changed the day I met him. I became part of something bigger. The man outside the window was the one who chased away the darkness and kept me safe. I didn't have to be afraid anymore.

Submerged in my thoughts, I was unaware of my father, Joseph, tapping on the glass. He's a tall, handsome man with distinguished gray hair that's always impeccably combed. He has a ruddy Irish complexion and a deep, commanding voice. Beneath the perfect exterior is a man with a temper that I feared.

Our eyes locked, and I flashed back to when I was five years old, experiencing his rage firsthand. I could usually tell when it was coming. First, his eyes would narrow and go blank. His jaw would clench, and his body grew rigid. Within seconds, objects were hurled through the air. Glass shattered, and furniture cracked. Sometimes his enormous hand would reach me before I was able to move. He would take me by the nape of my neck and launch me across the room. I landed in a crumpled heap and dared not say a word or even cry, fearing the next blow would be worse.

Joe and Jackie, my mother, have been divorced forever. They have always had a love-hate relationship. I was never daddy's little girl. The sun rose and set on my sister Sarah. The two of us lived with our mother, and Dad visited from time to time. Sometimes we spent the weekends with him, but Sarah never fell victim to his anger. She was associated with memories of a happier time. A time when they were a family, and their world was bright and full of possibilities. Not me. I was a constant reminder of their failed marriage. Although he had by no means been a driving force in my life, he was my father, and that deserved a certain amount of respect. I invited him to give me away in the family spirit, although I was not truly his to give.

When I let him in, he scooted next to me, taking my hand. His eyes, ordinarily distant and cold, were now filled with tears, and as he spoke, his voice trembled with emotion. If anyone saw our exchange, they would have thought we were engaged in a touching moment between father and daughter.

"Are you certain you want to go through with this, honey?"

"I have never been surer of anything in my life, Dad."

"If you don't want to, I will take you away. No one will say anything. If they do, they will have to deal with me." He raised his fist as if threatening anyone who would dare speak up.

The sentiment would have been even sweeter, if not so obviously rehearsed. It didn't come from the heart; I had his number.

Taking my cue, I kissed him on the cheek. "Thanks, Daddy, but there is no place I'd rather be." The day was a celebration. The prospect of my future exhilarated me.

When the time came for the ceremony to begin, the bridal party lined up and waited behind a row of neatly trimmed hedges where the guests could not see us. All the girls smiled at me, wished me the best, and were off. One by one, they disappeared down the aisle and out of my line of vision. Sarah was the last to leave. As she took her first step, the words, "Please don't go," escaped without permission from my mouth.

I reached out my hand to her, but she smiled the smile I knew so well, clicked her tongue twice, and said, "see ya' later, babe!" And she was gone.

She left, and the bridal march began. What else could I do? I bowed my head in prayer. "Dear God, help me to be a good wife. If I should be blessed with the gift of children, help me raise them well, and please, please, don't let me fuck this up. Amen."

With one last deep breath, I took the first step down the aisle. As I waited at the end of the pathway, the guests stood and turned my way. My heart was racing when my father took my arm.

"Are you ready, honey?"

I held on to him tightly. "Ready, Dad."

He led me down the rest of the way. Thank goodness he held me. I feared my knees would buckle, and I would end up flat on my face. For once in my life, he would be there to catch me if I fell.

Waiting at the end of the path flanked on either side by friends and relatives was my future husband, my best friend, the man who knew me better than any other. The one I trusted with all my heart. He waited for me. Watching me. Smiling at me. As impossible as it seemed, I think he was as happy as I was. My father shook his hand and placed mine in his. Grasping tightly, he led me up the three steps of the pavilion to the waiting minister.

Completely lost in the moment, the only thing I was focused on was the light in my future husband's beautiful green eyes. We were suspended in time, listening to the lilting music with notes that hung in the air, accompanied by the birds singing in the trees and the leaves' rustle. Neither of us said a word.

Once the music faded into the background, the minister read our vows. We focused on the words, giving the moment the utmost respect. Suddenly, right before we were to say 'I' do,' I succumbed to a case of giggles, which often strikes me at the most inconvenient times. I couldn't' rid myself of them. They boiled up on me like a pot of water about spew. Sarah must have seen the look on my face because I saw out of the corner of my eye that she was trying hard to hold back the laughter as well. One false move and all hell would break loose. If the first chuckle escaped, it would be insuppressible.

"Stop it, now," I murmured, so only those closest could hear me.

The laughter came in such a fit that everyone stared in disbelief. The tears rolled down her face as her body heaved with the strain of trying to regain her composure, but it was too late—the laughter was contagious.

I started to chuckle, as did Andrew, his brother David, and even my mother. What began as a case of the giggles became a wave of howling laughter rippling through the guests, gaining momentum with each person it passed. No one was safe.

Somehow, we managed to take each other for better or worse, in sickness and health, forsaking all others for as long as we both shall live. Andrew slipped the diamond band on my finger, and I placed a gold ring on his. Hearing the words, "Andrew, you may now kiss your bride," was all we needed to renew the laughter. Our Reverend Al then announced, "I am pleased to be the first to introduce the new Mr. and Mrs. Andrew Russo." Thunderous applause arose from the guests, whose eyes were wet with tears of joy and laughter.

Recounting the joy of our wedding day to Laura reminded me of how in love Andrew and I had once been——or at least how in love I was with him.

Chapter 7

WHEN LAURA ASKED ME to unleash the chaos that is Joe and Jackie on her, I glared at her with a half-smile and raised eyebrow. If you insist.

Mom, and I use the word mother loosely, is still a child herself, and parenting was a difficult task for her. Strange as it may sound, my mother had once been my world. I gladly would have given my life for hers. When I was little, I remember crossing the street with her. I would intentionally lag behind, believing that if a car would come and hit someone, it should be me—but that was a long time ago. Now, as an adult, some days, I wish she were dead. The word 'dead' lingered behind, making my soul shrivel in shame for even thinking it.

When I was about eleven, I asked her why she wasn't like the other mothers. "Well, darling, then I would be fat and boring like the cows in this town." She laughed at her joke. "Look at me. I'm still beautiful, sexy, and fun. You should be proud of me." She stood us in front of the mirror. "We look like sisters!

Besides, how many mothers can teach their daughter how to make a perfect martini?" She always thought she was so funny. "Remember, shaken, not stirred." I laughed despite not being amused.

Jackie is the only daughter of an extremely wealthy and ultra-conservative couple, born with a fire in her belly. At a young age, she declared war on the world around her. During her teen years, she openly despised both church and state or any institution trying to tell her what to do or how to act. She was a child of the sixties—only she was born in the forties. The irreconcilable differences between parents and child caused her parents to ship her off to boarding school. They hoped that someday their daughter would come around, but they were fooling themselves.

Jackie had always been beautiful and intelligent. She'd learned quickly how to use those attributes to her advantage. While in high school, Mom had an affair with one of her teachers just because she could. She'd wanted to experience what it was like to bring a grown man to his knees. In college, instead of studying, she'd found another way to pass. Unfortunately, one day the Dean had forgotten to lock his office door.

She was kicked out of school and cut off from the family financially. Fortunately, she had a beautiful singing voice, reminiscent of a young Judy Garland. She sang at the Bayou Club in Manhattan. The way she could mesmerize the audience was like casting a spell.

After a late business meeting, Joe stopped in one night and was instantly drawn into her web. He became a regular after seeing her the first time. The sexual tension between them smoldered for weeks. It was a dance of seduction performed with the eyes. Each song she sang was just for him. By the time they had their first date, their story's first chapter had already been written. The courtship was quick. Within six months, they were married. Two months after that, pregnant, and four years later divorced.

I was so young that I don't recall much of them being together. Sometimes I can catch a glimpse of some memories, none of them good. There was always lots of yelling and doors slamming. They went their separate ways. Sarah and I stayed with Mom, and Dad found himself a new wife.

Jackie loved us; of that, I'm sure, but we weren't her priority. My mother was the consummate party girl. It didn't have to be a holiday or formal celebration to break out the booze, pot, and cocaine. People came and went, enjoying the freedom and friendship they were able to find in our house.

Many mornings as a child, I woke to find empty scotch and wine glasses everywhere, while ashtrays overflowed with cigarette butts. Invariably, someone would be passed out in the middle of the living room.

"Mommy, who's that man sleeping on the couch?" I'd asked one morning.

"Oh, he's your Uncle Richie, honey."

"I don't have an Uncle Richie."

"You do now," she'd croaked with a raspy morning-after voice. "Be an angel and make Mommy a Bloody Mary. Remember, not too much Tabasco."

The person on the couch would stay for weeks, even months. Most of the time, they disappeared without so much as a goodbye.

On nights when she stayed home with us, Jackie would pour a large water glass full of cheap vodka and pop a sleeping pill or two. Some nights I would wake to a loud thump in the hallway; she would be out cold with an empty glass in one hand. No doubt, she fell on her way to make another drink.

"Mommy, wake up!" I'd yell while tapping her on the cheek, terrified she was dead. "Mommy, please get up." Once I checked, she was still breathing, I would use all my strength to hoist her to her feet and walk her back to bed.

"Come on, Mommy. Get under the covers."

"Oh, Julie, you're such a good girl. Thanks, honey," she'd slur and pat me on the face.

When I got back into bed, I prayed to God she would wake up in the morning.

As for Joe, honestly, I don't know very much. He never spoke about his childhood or his parents. Mom mentioned once that his mother and father died in a car crash when he was a teenager. He had two older brothers. One joined the Air Force right after the accident and was killed six months later in a training exercise. The other stayed to act as Joe's legal guardian.

When Dad turned eighteen, he joined the Navy as a fighter pilot. I don't think he witnessed much action firsthand. After his stint, he went to college on the GI bill, got a job, and met mom. Come to think of it, I never did meet his brother. As I said, I know very little.

Laura wanted to know, and now she may regret having asked.

48

Chapter 8

I REMEMBER MOM STANDING in her bathrobe, cigarette dangling out of her mouth, throwing around the pots and pans, screaming, "That bastard didn't send the money again!" When I would ask her what's the matter, she talked of child support and alimony, but if and when he sends it, it is never enough.

Eventually, we went on food stamps. I remember being humiliated every time we went to the grocery store. When we would get to the cashier, everyone stared at the colorful paper mom used and rolled their eyes. One time, I heard a woman whisper to her friend, "Watch your husband around that one. She is a divorcee; she'll steal your husband and your money."

Mom turned around and hissed, "You're just jealous, you old hag. Maybe I'll call your husband later." And she winked. Like I said, humiliating.

Dad would come to visit us when his new wife would let him. Sarah and I would sit by the window, anxiously awaiting the roar of his new Porsche announcing his arrival. Sometimes, he would take us both for a fancy lunch, but it was usually just Sarah. He called her princess and treated her like one, too. The visits were usually only a few hours. It would end with him giving her a big bear hug, lifting her off the ground. "You know I hate leaving you. Don't forget, who's my sunshine?" That was their thing. He asked the question, and she replied, "I am!" On the way out, he would tussle my hair and say, "Goodbye, little one."

I was seventeen when all the pieces finally came together. Mom was sitting in the kitchen drinking martinis with her friend Carol. I could tell by their hushed voices and audible gasps that they were in the middle of a very intense conversation. Being a nosey teen, I leaned up against the wall, out of sight but within earshot.

"Who knows about this, Jackie?" Carol whispered, but loud enough that I could hear.

"No one. I think Joe suspects, but I never confessed." Now I was really intrigued. I had to know what Mom was hiding.

"So, who's her father?"

For the sake of Laura's time, I gave her the abbreviated version. It goes something like this: Mom cheated on Dad when Dad started hitting her. She had some torrid affair with a stockbroker, got pregnant, got divorced, and here I am.

About a month after I overheard the conversation, I brought it up with Jackie. It's kind of messed up dinner conversation, so I asked straight out when I was making a snack. "Is Dad really my dad?" I couldn't bring myself to look at her.

"Why do you ask that?"

"I overheard you and Carol. It's okay. I've always known I was different. Just tell me the truth."

And she did. She gave me a name, an address, and a little backstory. Mom was known to embellish the truth, so I took it all with a grain of salt.

As for how this revelation affected me, my feelings were complicated. They still are. On the one hand, the man I have always known as my father is a violent asshole, and I am grateful none of his DNA courses through my body. On the other hand, he wasn't my biological father but never told me. He never even said he suspected that was the case. Yes, he treated me differently, even badly, but he didn't outright deny me. He has to get some credit for that. How could I hate him entirely? I can't, but I can resent the hell out of him.

I haven't ever reached out to my alleged biological father. A girl can only handle so much drama.

Chapter 9

AFTER THE WEDDING CEREMONY, we had a crazy reception. The hall we had chosen for our celebration was on the main thoroughfare that connected the towns where Andrew and I grew up. We spent much of our lives living less than 20 minutes apart, but it took over two decades to meet. I liked the thought that it was in God's plan all along; we were meant to be together.

Everywhere I looked, our guests were smiling, laughing, and having a wonderful time. My heart swelled with joy. It was not an extravagant affair. The room was sprinkled with intimate tables draped in fine linen, illuminated by candlelight. In the corner sat an oversized antique oak bar, a throwback from underground clubs during prohibition. The room appeared sophisticated and elegant, at least for the moment.

The euphoric cloud on which I floated was periodically interrupted by chants of, "shots, shots, shots!" This was the invitation of my newly acquired brother-in-law to head to the bar and down another pour of vodka. By mid-evening, Andrew was carried around by his merry band of brothers. He was tossed in the air like a life-sized rag doll.

My new adorable husband skated across the floor toward me, red-faced and shit-faced. At one point, he had donned a red bandanna, making him look like a pirate.

The time had come for the last dance of the evening. God knows he wasn't graceful, but he sure was able to make me smile.

"Hey, Mrs. Russo. Want to dance?" his words came out in one long string of consonants, grabbing my hand to lead me to the parquet dance floor.

"Sure, Mr. Russo. If you think you can."

He stumbled his way through *Heaven Knows* by Luther Vandross, and in the end, he brought me back for a dramatic grand finale. Leaning me into a low dip, he dropped me right on my ass. Once I got up, I kissed his pathetically drunk lips and whispered, "I love you, Mr. Russo."

"I love you too, Mrs. Russo. How's your beautiful ass?"

"Just fine, thank you. You can check it for bruises later," I said with a wink.

I wanted the night to go on forever, but unfortunately, it had to end. Everyone left with hugs and kisses. Our guests stood in the middle of the street or hung out of windows and sunroofs screaming their goodbyes and well wishes. Cars swerved, bringing traffic to a stop. There were many near misses. It could have been tragic, but we were all young, drunk, and indestructible.

Outside, our limousine waited to take us to our hotel, where we would spend our first night together as a married couple. We climbed in the back and opened the bottle of champagne that awaited. "To us!" he slurred.

"To the first day of a wonderful life together." I toasted back.

We rode to the hotel in silence, watching the neon lights of the highway rush by with my head on his shoulder. We were exhausted. That was when I heard the first snore of the evening.

We arrived at the Marriott Hotel right outside Newark International Airport. "Come on, honey," I whispered. I woke him gently with soft touches to his cheek. Slowly he opened his eyes, and, taking his hand, I led him through the corridors as though he was a young child. We arrived at our room and entered without the ceremonial carrying of the bride over the threshold. I considered myself lucky that I didn't have to carry him.

Once inside, I propped him up against the bed and began to remove his clothes. I unbuttoned his stiff white tuxedo shirt and pulled off the cuff links that his father had given him. I slipped the shirt from his shoulders and let it drop to the floor. I removed his belt, unbuttoned, and unzipped his pants. Slowly, I worked them down his legs. I leaned him to one side, allowing him to step out of them, but he lost his balance, tumbling onto the bed, bringing me with him. I landed on top of him and smiled, thinking this would be the moment. Leaning down, I pressed my slightly parted lips against his, but he had something entirely different on his mind.

"Baby, I got to eat. Let's order room service." He pushed me off and rolled to the side, picking up the phone without so much as glancing my way. He could barely see the numbers, but somehow managed to order. While we waited, we watched *The Godfather* for at least the hundredth time. An hour later, there was a knock at the door.

"Please don't get up, Andrew. I'll take care of it," I said with irritation.

The waiter brought in our order and placed it on the dresser. As I tipped him, Andrew began devouring his cheeseburger, french fries, and coke. I sat on the bed next to him, tucking my feet underneath, and ate my hot fudge brownie sundae. We fell asleep while Michael Corleone proved his loyalty to his family and gunned down Sallazzo and McCluskey in the Italian restaurant.

As I continued to relate these memories to Laura bit-by-bit, I found new revelations to confront, leaving me feeling exhausted.

Chapter 10

I WOKE AT FOUR o'clock in the morning, exhausted from the previous night's festivities. Andrew was sound asleep. I worked my way out of bed and into the shower. I stood under the warm running water, reliving the moment I officially became Mrs. Russo.

A few hours later, we boarded the plane to St. Bart's. After takeoff, Andrew announced, "Jul, I think I might puke." At once ordered two Bloody Marys in the hopes of not having our entire day ruined. We drank them down quickly and fell asleep until the final approach. By the time we landed, Andrew was a little less green.

The resort we chose was the kind of place usually reserved for the rich and famous. We were neither. We were driven to a small, thatched cottage with a rustic, unpolished door. The room was decorated in rich English antiques, and the fragrance of orchids permeated the air. We stood looking at each other with goofy smiles, knowing we were entirely out of our element. I ran across the room and jumped on the bed. I rolled around on what had to be the softest cotton sheets I had ever experienced. They were smooth as satin. I could imagine wrapping them around my naked body after making love. I called Andrew, "Get over here. You've got to see this." We had an amazing unobstructed view of the azure sea from the king-sized four-poster bed. Scanning the room, I admired the details. There was no radio or television. The only sounds were that of the local birds. In the far corner of the room was a doorway. I ran to see what treasure it hid.

There was a shower amid a beautiful, lush, tropical garden constructed to be half inside and half out, enclosed by seven-foot shrubbery for privacy. As I stripped off my travel clothes, a small green lizard ran over my barefoot; with "Holy shit!" erupting from my mouth, Andrew quickly came in.

"What's the matter?"

I was laughing so hard that I could barely get the words out. Crouching on the floor naked, I pointed my finger at the lizard that had decided to perch itself on the toilet seat. "Do you think it's potty trained?". Once our laughter subsided, I pressed my naked body against him and urged him toward the shower. "Come on," I said in my most sensual voice, grabbing his hands to escort him into our private rain forest.

Breaking free of my grip with unnecessary force, he snapped, "Jul, we just got here. There will be plenty of time for that later."

I stood stunned at his aggression, and then he softened. "Come with me." He led me to the large windows with plantation shutters and wrapped his arms around me. "Look at the water. I have never seen anything like that. I want to check out the beach. Don't you? Please, Honey. This feels like a dream."

"Okay." I backed off. In all fairness, I wasn't entirely disappointed. I was eager to see it as well, and he was right; there would be plenty of time to make love later.

We changed into our bathing suits and left through the sliding glass doors that opened directly onto the white powder sand. It was as delicious to go in the water as it was to look at, warm as a bath, and crystal blue. We dove as if dolphins and played like children until we were exhausted. We were the perfect honeymoon couple.

Our days were spent lazing on the beach, reading, holding hands, and soaking our bodies in the serene waters. We dined by candlelight, gazed lovingly into each other's eyes, and strolled arm in arm along the beach. No one looking at us would ever doubt our love.

We dined on lobster tails, truffle-mashed potatoes, and prosciutto-wrapped asparagus on our last night. We drank a bottle of 1988 Dom Pérignon in celebration. I raised my glass. "To my husband, you have made me the happiest woman on the face of the planet. Thank you for loving me."

"No, thank you, my wife," he said, and we clinked glasses.

Once our meal was over, we started the walk back to our room. "Honey, why haven't we made love since before the wedding?" He looked down, kicking at the sand, and shrugged. He kept walking without saying a word.

Chapter 11

"Looking back, can you see the pattern in his behavior?" Laura asked.

"Of course I do now, but I have never had an idea what a real relationship looks like. I sound like an idiot, but I honestly didn't know. For years, I have been trying to figure out how my life continues to end up in shreds. That's why I'm here."

After years of self-evaluation, I've come to realize I'm a person of extremes. When I'm happy, I'm on such a high that I'm untouchable and can hardly be kept earthbound. I soar with the birds and pin all my hopes on the belief that the euphoria will last forever. I'm so blinded by hope that I don't see the inevitable fall that follows.

Have you ever taken a walk in a summer rainstorm? The kind where the gutters can't take the water in fast enough and the streets become rivers? That's one of my favorite things to do. The rain comes down with such speed and force that it's cleansing. Standing outside in my bare feet, feeling my clothes saturate and my hair getting soaked, it's like a baptism. Everything gets washed away, temporarily. That is what happiness is for me. Momentarily, there is no past; I have been cleansed. The devil within has been eradicated.

Conversely, when I fall, I sink to such depths of despair. It's as if concrete blocks are tied to both of my feet, dragging me under life's dark, murky waters. Rarely do I have a middle ground. I am always walking the tightrope of sanity. I work hard to keep myself in line because I know I can easily tumble into a black abyss that I may never escape. I have stood by while my mother and sister lost themselves completely. I don't want the same thing to happen to me. I can't do that to my kids.

I have always been a walking dichotomy. I'm young and old; wise and dumb; strong and weak; loving and hateful; forgiving and vengeful; sane and insane. It's who I am. It's who I hate.

As much pain as I may be in, I can't even focus on it. I empathize so strongly with others that I feel an overwhelming responsibility for them. My job is to save everyone, whether they want me to or not. I have been that way for as long as I can remember. Maybe I subconsciously detected that something was going on within Andrew, and I wanted to help him.

No one would know by looking at me that I am struggling with who I am all the time, not even Andrew. I have an uncanny ability to give accurate advice to those who ask, and often wonder why I can't do the same for myself. The clarity I have for many others is completely lost when directed inward.

When Danni was getting divorced, I walked her through the entire process, never letting her beat herself up—never wavering in my faith in her. It might as well have been me getting divorced. I felt her sadness as if it were my own. I instinctively knew how to help her. When Kristy had breast cancer, we were on the phone daily, working through the all-consuming fear. When Sarah was in rehab, I always reminded her she was loved and worthy of a rich and sober life.

At the end of any given day, I am never satisfied with who I am. I lie in my bed and go over every word I have spoken, and every action taken. I find a way to blame myself for whatever is wrong in my life, or anyone else's for that matter. I'm not allowed faults, nor am I allowed to make mistakes. Of course, I make plenty of them and berate myself without mercy for each.

At various times in my life, I have wondered if people realize what they do and say can have a permanent and direct impact on someone else. Somewhere along the line, I became preoccupied with the concept of cause and effect, action, and reaction. These concepts became so ingrained in my psyche that I overanalyze everything.

I can be who everyone expects me to be during the day, but it is an entirely different story when night comes. No one knows the secret side of me, the part that deals with my demons.

When I close my eyes at night, the ability to shut off one of the most wounded parts of me no longer works. All the things I have put away in the deepest recesses of my mind creep up. No matter how hard I try to forget the past or shoo away the pain, it manages to find its way back. It is like an army of roaches crawling under the doorway of my mind, drawn to the silence and darkness of sleep. More often than not, I wake myself with screams and find my face wet with tears. The nightmares are always there, but they aren't the same. Sometimes I'm chased and pinned down by a shadowy figure. They sit on my chest and hold my arms down with their knees. They have their hand over my mouth, so I can't speak or yell for help. I thrash around, trying to remove the weight of their body on my chest, but I start to suffocate.

Sometimes I'm trapped like a rat in a cage, fighting to find a way out. There is a corridor, and I try to run as fast as I can to find an exit. With each step, my legs grow heavier until I cannot lift them, and I fall to the floor. I drag my body with my arms, clawing for every inch, digging my nails into the hard ground until they are shredded and bloody. There is always that faceless, nameless figure taunting me, knowing exactly what to say to rip my soul apart.

Some nights, I clench my teeth so tightly that I dream they are crumbling to dust or falling out from the pressure of my jaw. I stand with the pulverized remains of what had once been my teeth in my hands.

When I was 15, I had a dream I had died. I remember it as if it were yesterday, and it still scares me. I was at my high school, roaming the hallways in my light blue nightgown while everyone else was hustling off to homeroom. No one said hello or even acknowledged my presence. I reported to class as everyone else did and took my seat. During regular announcements, they said I had died. The service and burial would take place in the school atrium. I knew it couldn't be true. After all, I was sitting right there, but no one was able to see me. I screamed and yelled, trying to tell them I was alive, but no one heard me.

Everyone filed outside and stood beside my grave. I followed their gaze to my unmoving body in the deep trench below. My art teacher, Mr. Meyers, looked my way. He could see me. He realized that if I was visible to him, there most certainly had to be a mistake. He agreed to perform a test to make sure I did not belong in the afterworld and could take my place back among the living. He stuck the sole of my foot with a sharp metal pin, and when I reacted, he had his confirmation. He ran to stop the burial, but it was too late. We looked on helplessly as the dirt was shoveled upon my body; heaping mounds landed upon my unmoving body. Maggots crawled out of my eyes, nose, and mouth. Right before I disappeared into nothingness, I awoke. As in all my dreams, I was rarely heard, and as usual, no one was able to rescue me.

Despite what some may think, I greet each morning with joy. Seeing the sunlight means another night of horrors would be chased back into the blackness of my inner mind. I wouldn't have to face the night for at least another twelve peaceful hours. I wipe away the tears and shower off all the disgust that drapes me like a cloak, dress, and leave it behind. I have no room for that in the daylight. Every day begins with the same phrase, "Today I'm going to be happy."

Chapter 12

"ARE YOU AWARE OF what causes that extreme sense of empathy and pain you describe?" Laura questioned in our next session.

"I'm crazy?" I was half-joking.

"What you are describing sounds like a form of post-traumatic syndrome. Recent studies have shown that many people who demonstrate extreme empathy were products of dysfunctional homes and childhood trauma. Those experiences may have worn down the natural defense system you were born with, therefore leaving you more in tune with others that may be suffering."

"I suppose that makes sense."

"Were there other incidents of violence outside of your father?"

I most certainly did not want to go there, but if I had any hope of straightening out my life, I didn't have a choice.

I had always yearned to have a normal life. One where I wasn't the youngest daughter of the divorcee who showed up at parent-teacher conferences with the sharp smell of scotch on her breath and her cleavage out for public consumption.

My sister, however, is my complete opposite. Like my mother, she is tall and leggy, with an ample bosom always highlighted in her tight shirts. When Sarah was old enough, she and Mom became best friends and often went on the 'hunt' together. They had a connection—an understanding that Mom and I didn't have. I didn't fit in. I was a freak in my family, an outsider. Jackie often joked that she would've sworn I was adopted if she hadn't seen me come out of her body.

I longed to be protected against the trouble that seemed to always be invited into our house. Whether it was exposure to drugs and alcohol or to one of Jackie's friends who didn't know his limitations—especially when it came to appropriate attention to little girls. I was never comfortable in a place that should've been my safe space.

One year, Jackie had one of her infamous parties on Christmas Eve. At least sixty people had jammed into our small two-bedroom red-brick ranch house on North Cottage Drive. Sarah and I had worn our matching floral flannel nightgowns and peeked at the gathering from our bedroom door. Everyone kissed each other on the cheek, laughed, and called each other darling. The party looked very glamorous to us. Jackie was always radiant with her long jet-black hair, dressed in a tight red jumpsuit that enhanced her zaftig curves. The zipper was down to her navel, and a long gold chain draped from her neck. She was a knockout, no doubt about it.

She basked in the glory of adoration; it was as if she were holding court. Sarah and I would pretend that we were at our own party, and men adored us. "Oh, Sarah, you look fabulous," I would speak in my most proper English accent.

She would respond, "So do you, Darling. You just get better looking each time I see you." We rolled on the floor laughing and played until we could no longer keep our eyes open, despite the loud music and noise in the next room.

I woke sometime later that night to the pressure of a person's body on top of me. His prickly beard and mustache scratched my face, and his wet mouth covered mine. His hot thick tongue was forcing its way into my mouth while his hands were looking for a way under my nightgown. My eyes burst open, and I tried to scream, but it was muffled. There was no need for him to hold me down. The pressure of his body pinned my small preadolescent frame without any effort.

Before I thought I would die of fright, the door burst open, flooding the room with light. Thank God! I thought. Mommy would save me. I had such an overwhelming sense of relief that I started to cry. I waited for Mom to call the police, yell, scream, hit him, do something—anything to show her outrage—but instead, without alarm in her voice, she asked what was going on. The man with the beard responded with a sly smirk, "We're playing adult games." then he squeezed the area just above my knee, making me jump.

Jackie snickered, "Come along now, let the child sleep. You need to behave yourself. You're mine, you dirty old man." With that, she slapped his ass. As they left the room, my mother called over her shoulder, "That's what happens when you play with the big boys; now go to sleep." She closed the door behind her. As soon as she was gone, I curled up into a tight ball and rocked myself to sleep. The only thought I remember having was that I wanted to go home. I didn't know where that was or what it meant, but I wanted desperately to go home.

I'd love to say that was the only time something like that happened, but it wasn't. When I was eleven, my mother befriended a young man named Jerry, whom she had met at the grocery store. He was twenty and drove a royal blue Pontiac Grand AM. He was tall and heavy with a short crop of dark hair and eyes that were dark as ink. He was an odd boy whose eyes darted around as he spoke, never landing in the same place twice. As mom had done with so many others in the past, she took him in and made him part of our family.

He made me very uneasy from the beginning. His eyes burned through me as I walked around the house, but when I tried to catch him, he would stare into a corner, pretending he hadn't been looking at all. One day I came home from school; no one was home except him. He was watching television in my mother's room...in her bed. I snuck past, hoping he wouldn't notice, and went into the room I shared with my sister. Within moments, Jerry barged in and plopped down on my bed with a groan.

"What are you doing?" he bounced up and down on my mattress.

"My homework," I hissed, dripping sarcasm.

"Let me see. You know, I'm really smart." He snatched the book out of my hands and started flipping through the pages.

"No, that's okay. Could you please leave my room? I have a ton of work to do." I tried to sound polite with my hand out for him to return my textbook.

"Not until we have a tickle fight." That was when he began grabbing at me. He started with my sides and then my legs. I squirmed and screamed. It may have sounded as if I was laughing at someone standing outside of my room, but I wasn't. I knew what was about to happen. After it happens once, you start to get a sense of these things. It was not going to happen again. It couldn't. I wanted him to stop, but of course, he didn't. I flipped around like a fish out of water, and then he ripped at the button of my jeans and began to pull with such force the button popped off, and the zipper broke. My pants split down the seam, exposing my pink panties with the day of the week on them. As much as I tried, I couldn't hold him off. He took his large hand and grabbed at my most personal spot.

"No!" I screamed repeatedly. "No, get off! Get off!" I kept fighting and kicking at him with my heel until he finally let go. I pushed myself as far away as possible, bracing my back against the wall with my legs drawn tight.

When he got up and straightened his shirt, his face looked distorted, and his eyes were black and narrow. He bent over my shaking body, took my head in his hands, and brought his mouth against my ear as if to tell me a secret, "Tell anyone, and I'll kill you, you fucking little cunt, and when I'm done with you, I'll do your mother and sister."

With that, he threw my head back so hard my brain rattled, and he left my room. Once he was gone, I changed my torn jeans and ripped panties. The bruises had already started to appear around my thighs, and the scratches had begun to swell. His body odor clung to me. The smell ripped at my insides just as he tore at my outside.

I could not understand why this happened. I figured either I was making too much of it, and it happened to everyone, or it was my fault, and I brought it on myself. Maybe I was a tease. Perhaps I deserved it. It didn't matter because I was never the same after that.

As the years went by, I felt as if there was never enough oxygen for me to catch my breath. All I wanted was some peace. I wanted Jackie to be like the other mommies. I wanted her to come home at night to tuck me in. I wanted her to protect me from the insanity in the world—but there would be no protection, no escape. So, I never told, and no one ever cared enough to ask.

After disclosing these memories to Laura, she asked, "Julie, do you have any friends? The kind you can confide in?"

"Not in this life—Julianne's life. I have lots of acquaintances. I might even call them friends, but not in the truest sense of the word. It's all very superficial. That being said, I do. I have a few close ones who are near and dear to my heart. They are part of 'my circle.' I couldn't have gotten this far without them." I smiled, thinking of the girlfriends I grew up with.

"Are they aware of what you endured?"

"They know a little bit. They saw firsthand some outrageous events. I remember once we were sitting in the kitchen rolling a joint when Jackie walked in. All the girls froze except for Kristy, who threw herself on top of the weed. Mom walked by and perched herself upon the counter wearing her flimsy see-through nighty, 'I am horribly insulted that you girls… didn't offer me a hit.' I was mortified."

Of course, my friends giggled because they were relieved she wasn't going to bust us. They thought it was amazing that I had such a cool mom. I thought it was a disgrace. As far as the other stuff, the only one who knows a little is Danni, and that is just because her family is incredibly fucked up, too.

Laura asks me to tell her about Danni, so I begin a stroll down memory lane, relaying my history with my best friend. "She is my confidant, my go-to for anything that I have to let out. I don't tell her the gory details, but she knows enough to get me.

We met when we were in elementary school. I remember seeing her on the swings all alone, staring at the dirt below her feet. She looked so sad, and my heart ached for her. As I approached, I noticed she had a large black eye.

"Hi, are you okay?" I winced.

"Yeah, why?" She barked with hostility, as if I dared to speak to her.

"Your eye. The bruise looks like it hurts." She glared at me.

"It's okay. Do you want to see mine?" I lifted the back of my pink Micky Mouse t-shirt, exposing the fading green bruise Joe had left behind during his last visit.

That was our defining moment. I recognized in her the undeniable pain we shared. I jumped on the swing next to her, and we became inseparable. When her father would go on a tear, she would escape out the backdoor and run to my house. My house may have been crazy, but at least when dad wasn't around, no one was kicking the shit out of anyone.

Chapter 13

"JULIE, WERE THERE ANY adults you could tell? I know you had a terrible relationship with your mother and father, but what about grandparents, aunts, uncles?" Laura inquires.

I continued to relay my past as if I were dictating my biography to this woman, whom I hadn't known for long, yet I confided some of my darkest secrets to her.

I had Grandparents. Not the kind that rolled around on the ground to play or gave loads of hugs and kisses, but I loved them. I could never let them know what was going on. They were not those kinds of people.

My mom, Jackie, hated her parents. The way they dressed and ate. Their life was filled with an order that gave it a kind of grace. Going to their Greenwich, Connecticut home was my refuge. I loved to walk through the formal gardens to watch the butterflies land on the echinacea or sit poolside and drink freshly brewed iced tea garnished with a sprig of newly picked mint from the herb garden. I would dangle my feet in the water as the elegant plastic swans danced around the pool, choreographed by the breeze.

My grandparents would take me to the New York City Ballet or the latest Broadway show on my visits. Sometimes it was an art exhibit that was all the rage. I had seen the New York Philharmonic perform by age five and had been to the Plaza so often the staff addressed me by name. We dined at the finest restaurants in Manhattan and shopped at Saks Fifth Avenue and Neiman Marcus.

Grandmother and I would enter the 'young ladies' department to purchase my annual spring dress. "Look, ladies, Julianne is here," squealed one of the women loudly. Before I could say anything, I was surrounded by three ladies leading me to the dressing room.

Janie, the one in charge, bent down so we were eye to eye. "What will it be today, sweetheart?"

Grandmother was swaddled in a mink stole clasped together with a jewel-encrusted bumble bee broach. I looked over at her for an answer. "We are going to Swan Lake tomorrow. I would like her to be dressed appropriately."

With a flick of her wrist, the women began to strip me down to my undergarments. They began redressing me in the latest fashion season with all the accessories as if I were a porcelain doll.

In hindsight, I realize I was being groomed to be the little lady my grandparents always hoped my mother would be. I was her replacement. I didn't mind. When I was with them, my life was peaceful. After our daily adventures, I would sleep in a queen-sized bed complete with silk sheets, a hand-stitched satin quilt, and pillows that were soft enough to be clouds. On the nightstand sat a pitcher of water and a glass if I got thirsty during the night. I would sleep and dream. Not the usual nightmares—I would have beautiful, happy dreams. One of my favorites was when I was a ballet dancer. I would glide elegantly across the long wooden stage. I was the picture of grace and beauty. After performing a complex variation spotlighting my unparalleled technique, the audience rose to their feet, exploding into cheers of 'Bravo!' Roses were tossed onto the stage, and I could feel the love surrounding me.

Being with Grandma and Grandpa was the opposite of my life at home. I dreaded when our visits came to an end.

"Grandma, may I please stay one more day?" I would beg.

"I'm sorry, my darling, but Grandfather and I are not equipped to care for a little girl. Even one as lovely as you, dear," she stroked my cheek softly with her weathered hand.

"Please, Grandmother! Please! Don't make me go." I could feel the tears spring to my eyes.

Grandma's soft side disappeared. "Now, Julianne, do not raise your voice. That is not the way a young lady behaves. You will go home with your mother. You may return next month."

"Yes, Grandmother." I dutifully grabbed my suitcase with my head hung low. I cried all the way back home, where chaos reigned.

Between visits with my grandparents, I found a way to escape without ever leaving the house. I got lost in television. It was the only place that could take me far away without going anywhere at all. I lived in a world of perfect families who were able to resolve their problems in half an hour. Shows like *The Partridge Family*, *The Nanny*, *The Professor*, *Please Don't Eat the Daisies*, and my personal favorite, *The Brady Bunch*. How I longed to be a Brady—Cindy Brady, more specifically. Although a pain to her older siblings, Cindy was the youngest; the older siblings were always there for her. Her parents imparted wisdom that would help her through the hard times. Alice, the housekeeper, always had a hot, delicious meal at the ready. That was the dream.

Everything changed when my grandparents moved west to San Francisco. Grandpa retired and had always dreamed of living in 'The Golden State.' They packed all the things they valued, except for me. They left me with my mother and sister and didn't look back. I had been abandoned. That's how I saw it.

I wasn't a beautiful girl, but I was slightly above average. In high school, I was skinny, awkward, and shy. I had never wanted to call attention to myself. I liked being a nameless face at school. I didn't date much, and I was still a virgin—one of the few left at my age and something that meant a lot to me. I drifted along in obscurity or did so as much as possible, given the Brennan's reputation. Regardless of how I tried not to, eventually, I became a product of my environment. The time had come to learn how to live in a world that made me horribly uncomfortable.

The women in my family have what we refer to as the 'it' factor. My grandmother, mother, and sister had 'it,' and surprisingly, so did I. I learned how they wielded their power. Some girls learned ballet, some studied literature, but I became proficient in the art of seduction.

I was able to manipulate my way out of class or skip school entirely. I could get away with almost anything, as long as the person in charge was a man. It was in the voice, a glint in the eyes, and the suggestive tilt of the hips. The manipulation was subtle, but incredibly effective. I had a sense of power I had never felt before. Finally, I had control over something.

When I was seventeen, I started dating Bobby Pierson. He'd graduated the year before and commuted to Rutgers, our local university. When we were in school together, he had been the gorgeous, popular, star quarterback and captain of the football team. He, of course, dated the captain of our cheer squad. He never even glanced my way the year before, but that changed when we met again at the homecoming football game.

I was rooting for my team with the rest of the cheerleading squad when I realized Bobby was looking at me from the sidelines. Our eyes locked, and he gave me a charming, irresistible smile. At first, I thought I was mistaken. I looked behind me, checking to see if someone else was standing there, but no one was. The smile was meant for me. I went a little weak in the knees. After the game, he caught up to me as I was leaving the field.

"Hey, you're Julie, right?"

I nodded. I was so nervous that I'd lost all ability to speak.

"Any chance you're free tonight? My buddy's having a party, and I'd love for you to come."

I had gone from a virtual nothing to having the attention of the guy every girl wanted. Once I regained my power of speech, I happily agreed, and that was when we began to date. He was funny, charming, and popular. What girl would say no?

The following month, I was at his house, and we sat kissing on his parent's couch. They were deep, passionate kisses that became more intense with each minute. My jeans were already unbuttoned, as were his, when he leaned over me, putting us in a compromising position. The hardness in his pants pushed against me.

"I'm sorry, Bobby, but I can't do this. I'm still a virgin," I meekly told him.

"Really? I don't believe you!" he sniggered in surprise.

"Well, it's true. I've never done it and don't think I'm ready. I want to wait until I'm married. Kind of corny, huh?"

"It's sweet. I think it's adorable you want to wait. Don't worry. It's cool." He winked.

After three months, we were still together. One Saturday night, we went to a party, and both drank far too much. We stumbled our way back to his house and passed out on his living room floor.

A short while later, I woke up with him on top of me. It took me a moment to focus and figure out what was happening. His body was shifting in a motion that I recognized was not okay as his penis thrust inside me.

"What the hell are you doing?" I pushed at his shoulders to remove him from my body.

"Oops, sorry. Too late." He groaned as he pulled out. I could feel his cum running out of me. Quickly, I scrambled to find my panties and shorts and ran the two miles to my house. I snuck into my room, not wanting to wake anyone, and curled up in my bed. I rocked myself all night, not understanding what just happened or why.

The next day, my crotch was throbbing and sore from him, forcing himself into my unconscious body. I began to realize sex had no real meaning. It wasn't romantic or loving, as it appeared on television or in books. As my sister says, that is a fantasy. Sex is an aggressive act. An act of power, and I was done being powerless.

From that day on, I would find a man to make me feel better when I was down. I drew their attention in that family way. With a lick of the lips and a sideways glance, I was bathing in the excitement of the hunt until my mood lifted. Unfortunately, the high was fleeting. When the adrenaline rush of playing the game ended, I crashed hard. I ended up in a state of despair and a place of absolute loneliness until I got another fix. That's how the cycle fed on itself for years.

I could get a man to want me, maybe even beg for me, but the one thing I couldn't do was keep him.

I had never been taught how to do that. It could be because my teacher didn't know herself.

The empty sexual encounters left me drained, physically and emotionally. I wanted desperately to be in love, or at least be loved. I wasn't the vixen I portrayed. But it was the only time I felt in control.

What I wanted was storybook love, love song love, Carol and Mike Brady love.

I tried many times to have a real relationship, but it never worked. Either I exposed my vulnerabilities too early and was marked as easy prey, or I was too sensual and seen as a slut.

Many of the men I had chosen to fall for were emotionally unavailable. Maybe I thought I could be the one to fix them. When I was doing something for them, I did not have to think about myself, and how truly screwed up I was. Ultimately, they always left me, or I pushed them away. I'm not sure I could tell the difference.

Chapter 14

I took two weeks off from seeing Laura. Part of therapy was helping, but part of it was killing me. No matter how I tried, nothing made any sense. The only thing I knew with absolute certainty was that I adored my children.

I loved holding them in my arms when they slept. I was astounded by the miracle of their existence that I created something perfect while being so imperfect. When I closed my eyes, I could still remember the feeling of holding Jack right after he was born. As soon as I took him in my arms, I studied his perfect, intricate ears for hours. When I looked at them, I was sure I believed in God. How else could such details come to be? My children are what I had waited for my whole life. I wanted time to stop so I could hide in my little corner and hold them forever.

Looking around the room, I was reminded of how naïve I was when we bought the house.

The wedding came and went... three, six, nine months passed, but the sex never got better, and he grew more distant. He had endless meetings and conferences to attend. He even missed my birthday. Andrew wasn't mean or abusive; he just wasn't there. Physically or emotionally.

One Sunday morning, I tiptoed into his office, giving a slight cough to get his attention.

"What's up?" He asked without looking up.

"Babe, what's going on?" I was trying to sound as non-confrontational as possible. "Have I done something to upset you?"

"No. Of course not. I'm busy. That's all."

"Well, it's just that you're busy ALL THE TIME."

"Julie, stop it!" Andrew pushed back in his chair and slammed down his pen. "I'm trying to get everything in order so I can buy you your little house with a white picket fence. Just like you've always wanted. I can't do that if I sit around on my ass all day, now can I?"

He was right. I was acting like a baby. He was away so much because he loved me. Doesn't everyone want to be loved that way? I still found myself wondering about the sex. He never gave me a reason for that.

As Andrew worked, I made housing spreadsheets and files that included information on towns, school statistics, the percentage of children who go to college, median income, average home prices, transportation methods, train schedules, and even the average number of children per household.

After three months of intense house hunting, my realtor, Kathy, took me to see a house that had come on the market the night before.

"Julie, if you like this one, there is no time to waste. The market is hot, and the owners are looking for a quick sale. If this doesn't work for you, I'm afraid I am out of options. We have seen everything."

"Why are they selling? The price seems very low. Is there something wrong with it?" I asked as we drove to the house.

"It seems the owners are splitting up. Rumor has it they had a screaming match on the front porch last week. Infidelity, I think."

"Really? How very sad." As a newlywed, it was hard for me to wrap my head around a spouse cheating.

"From what I hear, the wife was telling the husband to go 'you know what' his assistant, and he called her cold and frigid. It was ugly. They weren't even married for two years!" she exclaimed.

"How do you know all this?" I snipped incredulously.

"Small town gossip. You can't keep anything private in Mayberry," she giggled.

I found nothing funny about it.

We pulled up in front of a neglected turn-of-the-century Victorian house sitting proudly at the top of a knoll. It was white with off-kilter black shutters. It proclaimed its strength as having endured over one hundred years. When looking at it, I couldn't help but wonder how many families had lived here and what stories remained in the rooms.

The stone steps led to a warped wrap-around front porch with missing boards. Sitting in the middle was a nine-foot-tall oak door with a round cast-iron knocker. It was regal.

Before walking in, I could see the ghosts of the anger that played out weeks before. I could envision them, the couple I had never met. He looks off in the distance; she is standing alone with tears streaming down her face. My heart fell just a bit. I was intruding on their moment of pain. Before getting too carried away, I put it where I store all the things that would be dealt with at another time and continued into the house.

We walked into the foyer, which was trimmed in original chestnut molding. The floor was honey oak with inlays of rich mahogany, making a checkered pattern of sorts. They were scratched and scuffed from years of passage, but there was no denying the master craftsmanship that turned it out. Off the foyer sat a small parlor with floor to ceiling windows with rope sashes that would carry the wavy glass panes up or down. It was easy to envision where perhaps a Victrola or harpsichord may have sat. In my mind, I could see the family. The father smoking a pipe in a rocking chair, the mom doing needle-point that read 'Bless This House,' as the children, a boy, and a girl, sat on the floor playing Chinese checkers.

I had stepped into a beautiful, romantic past that beckoned me to join them. As we walked from room to room, I hardly noticed the cracks in the windows and stained carpet. I only saw what it could be. I wanted to restore it to its former glory. I wanted to save it.

Quickly, I drove to our brownstone. When I arrived, I excitedly bounced up all thirty-six stairs, bursting open the door when I got to the top. "Hurry up, get your coat. We have to get to Ridgewood before it's gone! I found it!"

There was no answer.

"Andrew? Where are you?" I walked down the short hallway and found him sitting in front of his computer.

"Are you okay, babe?" He was red and sweaty. No response. "Baby, are you okay?" He had a strange look in his eyes that would later become familiar to me.

Suddenly, he snapped out of it. "Oh yeah. It's this fucking computer." He cursed, smacking at the top of his screen. "It's a piece of shit!"

The monitor was blank. "Did you check all the cables?"

"Of course, I'm not an idiot."

"What can I do?" I asked, rubbing his tense shoulders.

"No, don't worry about it. What are you so excited about?"

I took out the flier of the house. "Check this out," I said and waited a moment for a reaction. When none was forthcoming, I proceeded to give him a detailed description, "It has four bedrooms, one and a half baths, wraparound porch, and best of all, a working fireplace in the primary bedroom. Can you imagine it, honey? Lazing in bed with a roaring fire, sipping hot coffee and reading the paper?" When I saw my approach wasn't working, I quickly switched gears. "I know it's more expensive than we'd planned, but if we do the work ourselves, it will be a sound investment. Think about this; in two years, we could probably clear thirty thousand dollars, which is solely based on current market conditions. Sounds like a solid investment, huh?"

"Okay, okay!" He threw his hands up in mock surrender. "We'll go first thing tomorrow. You win."

"No, we need to go today. It might be gone tomorrow. Please, we have to go now."

"I told you, we will go tomorrow. Stop worrying so much. It will still be there." The tone in his voice strongly suggested that it was futile to argue. I reluctantly agreed.

The following day, we drove to Ridgewood. Kathy was leaning against her Audi, waiting for us outside the house.

"You're lucky, Julie. I just got off the phone with the listing agent, and it's still available, but she thinks an offer is coming in today, so we'd better hurry." She glanced over to Andrew, "Hi! Glad you could join us. If you're both ready, let's go inside."

I could tell by the look on Andrew's face he was less than thrilled with the house. Sure, the peeling paint and rotting wood could be intimidating. One might call it rundown if one wanted to be cynical, but that would only apply if one didn't have the vision. I had enough for both of us.

As soon as we entered, he commented on the peeling wallpaper and smelly carpet. He pointed out every fault. As we walked from room to room, he went ahead to deconstruct everything.

"Jul, this place is a dump! I can't believe you want to take on a project like this." The disgust in his voice came through loud and clear.

"It's not a dump!" I was offended by his choice of words. "It has been neglected, but if you look closely, you'll see it is a diamond in the rough."

After an hour of looking at plumbing, electrical, and heating issues, I lost all hope the house would ever be mine.

He turned to me as we were heading for the door, "Jul, this house is more than I can handle right now." He must have seen my eyes go glassy as I fought back the tears that were ready to breach my bottom lids. His mouth twisted as he glanced around. "The molding looks original, and I suppose once we ripped out the cat-stained carpet and put on a fresh coat of paint, it could be decent. This is against my better judgment, but tell me, do you really love it?" He cocked his head, and a crooked smile took the place of his grimace.

I screamed, "Yes! Oh, my God, yes!"

Andrew nodded at Kathy, "You heard the little lady; write it up."

I jumped into his arms and wrapped my legs around him. "Thank you, thank you so much, Honey. I love you." I smothered him with kisses. "This is going to be wonderful. You'll see. I'm going to give you the greatest home. I promise."

Ninety days later, we were ripping out carpet, sanding floors, and refitting doors. Every day we came home after work, put on our old jeans, t-shirts, and work boots, and tore the house apart before slowly rebuilding it room by room. We worked side by side for one full year. Together, we turned a decrepit and dank house into a beautiful home filled with sunlight and pride of ownership. We brought it alive again.

Going into our third year of marriage, Andrew received a promotion and became the Assistant Director in his department. The firm where I still worked was busier than ever.

I had started to make some friends, which was never easy for me, but my life was different now. I traded in my oversized sweatpants for designer workout gear and cut my hair into a suburban bob. We purchased a new BMW coupe, and I began to introduce myself as Julianne.

Our lives were full, and at the end of the evening, we would crawl into bed together and fall asleep from sheer exhaustion. Often, I would reach over to him and place a kiss on his lips; sometimes, it would lead to sex, but most of the time, he pulled away with the same excuses I had gotten used to hearing.

I began to wonder, had I gotten ugly? Was I a huge disappointment? Maybe he didn't love me anymore. Many nights I cried myself to sleep, but he never noticed.

No question about it; we were growing apart. When I spoke to him, he never showed any reaction or emotion. If I had told him I'd robbed the local bank, the same expression would likely be on his face.

We no longer could read what the other one wanted without having to use words. There were no sideways glances of anticipation for an evening of romance, no smiles to let the other know they were loved. I couldn't remember the last time he touched me, complimented me, or even sat in the same room with me for more than thirty minutes.

I grew tired of being ignored and insisted we talk. "Please, Andrew, tell me what's going on. I don't understand what is happening to us." I cried, begging for an explanation.

He kissed me on the forehead. "Nothing is going on. I have a lot on my plate. Call Danni and make plans to go out tomorrow night. I think you need to get out of the house. You need to find something else to keep you occupied instead of worrying so much." With that, he walked away. He was patronizing me, and it was pissing me off.

Around that same time, Andrew began to control our finances. I was locked out of our joint bank account. He decided where we went, who we saw, and what we bought. Somehow, I had lost my voice, or perhaps I had surrendered it. I stopped speaking up. It seemed that everything I said and did was wrong. I didn't know who this man was. He certainly was not the same person with whom I had fallen in love. He had become a stranger with whom I had no connection.

On the few nights he made it home in time for dinner, he never liked what I made. He would hurl comments my way like, "When are you going to learn how to make a decent gravy, Jul? I gave you Mama's recipe. Why aren't you using it?" or "This is too bland. You need to start using more spices. You need lessons from Mama." His voice was patronizing.

I wanted to scream, "Then go home to Mama!" But I didn't. As usual, I kept quiet, afraid of upsetting him.

He was always in a lousy mood and pessimistic about everything. In his world, the glass was perpetually half empty. I felt like a failure, and he had turned into a grumpy old man. I was losing myself, along with my pride.

Growing tired of waiting on him and begging for attention, I decided that revolving my life around him wasn't working. It was demeaning to have to beg my husband to make love to me. It was time to concentrate on what I wanted for a change. This was when I first started to think about leaving. In my ambition to be the perfect wife, I had lost myself.

Andrew was always working late, so one night, I figured it was the perfect opportunity to learn how to 'surf the net.' It gave me something other to do than sit around wallowing in self-pity—besides, I didn't have any ice cream in the house.

I went into his office, his inner sanctum in which I was never allowed, plopped down in his padded chair, and spun around, taking in my surroundings. There was no question; it was his room. The walls covered in concert posters, sports memorabilia, and shelves upon shelves of books on computers, accounting, and every Tom Clancy novel ever written, screamed of him. No sign of me was evident in the room.

As I dug around his desk, I found one small picture of us tucked away that had been taken on our first vacation together. We went to Cabo San Lucas, Mexico. The photo was taken upon our return from a day of horseback riding, swimming with manta rays, and parasailing. We were throwing back a shot of tequila to celebrate our death-defying experiences.

"Here's to a wonderful vacation," I'd toasted.

"Here's to you, sweetheart. I love you," he said softly.

The look in his eyes made me feel so unbelievably loved. I still have the terra cotta shot glasses somewhere in the hall closet. I smiled at the memories while booting up the computer. It was surprisingly easy. Slowly, I worked my way through the browser, learning how to find and open files. There was a listing for bookmarks, so I clicked on it. A second screen dropped down, displaying pages that had been saved. I found *ESPN*, *Wall Street Journal*, *Urban Myths*, *Hot Asian Babes*, *Blondes with Boobs*, and *Wet Willing Women*.

It dawned on me; that they were porn sites. I laughed out loud. "No, fucking way," I mumbled. The thought of my husband looking at porn was absurd. He had turned into one of the most sexually uptight and repressed people I had ever known. Honestly, I didn't even think he liked sex anymore.

I opened the files, clicking on them randomly. The screen displayed various nude women in explicit poses. "Well, I guess Andrew still has a sex drive. It's just me he's not attracted to." I scoffed at the realization.

I realized that I didn't know him nearly as well as I had thought. The man I knew was strictly vanilla ice cream in the lovemaking department. No sprinkles or toppings of any kind. Missionary. No oral. Little to no foreplay and never, ever any toys.

The pornography itself was not the problem, but porn in place of sex was. We had not made love in six months. Not only did it make me angry, but it also raised questions I couldn't answer. The obvious one is, why? And had he gone past the stage of voyeurism into actual human contact?

I wandered around the house aimlessly, wondering what to do next. I decided to head to the train station in hopes of catching him when he disembarked. Since I didn't know when he was coming in, I sat for two hours, growing more irate with each passing minute. When I spotted him, I waved at him, beckoning him to the car. He greeted me with a peck on the cheek, "Hey babe, how are you? How'd you know what time I was coming in?"

"I didn't. I've been waiting for you," I said without looking at him.

Before he had a chance to snap in his seatbelt, I unleashed everything.

"What the fuck are you doing on your computer? Are you some kind of fucking freak? Can you only get off looking at porn?" The disgust in my voice was evident.

He sat in the passenger side of the car, looking blankly at me. It was the same look I had become familiar with over our years together.

"Well?" Nothing in his eyes or face showed what he was thinking, or even if he heard me. His continued silence and complete lack of emotion triggered my rage. I punched the steering wheel with both hands. "What the fuck are you doing? Are you cheating on me?"

"No, of course not!" He gave a convincing impression of someone appalled at the mere suggestion of infidelity.

"Then why don't you touch me anymore?" I snapped back.

"I don't know."

"God, you're so fucking full of shit, Andrew!" As I growled, he continued to stare blankly at me. I wanted to slap his face, but instead, I stepped on the accelerator and tore out of the parking lot, leaving behind a cloud of dust and some kicked-up gravel.

Not a word was uttered on the ride home. I stormed inside, slamming the door behind me. I wasn't about to repeat history and have the town gossip about us like the previous owners.

He followed behind, acting sullen and whipped. I glared at him in disgust. "You look like a little boy caught with nudie magazines under his bed by his mother. Man up and tell me what is going on."

"Nothing is going on. I'll stop. I promise. I haven't done anything. Don't be upset. It doesn't mean anything." He insisted, reaching out to me, but I shook him off and went upstairs to bed.

He came in hours later, snuggled up to me. "I love you, babe. Don't worry about a thing. It's going to be okay." He kissed my shoulder.

I replayed the evening repeatedly during the night, tossing and turning until exhaustion won and I drifted off. In the morning, I woke up to the savory smell of freshly brewed chicory coffee. Following the aroma, I found my favorite mug warm to the touch and a small bowl of blackberries sitting on my nightstand. Alongside sat a simple handwritten note, "Good morning, my love." Maybe I was over reacting... again. I decided to let it go.

Chapter 15

"I'm happy to see you, Julie. Is everything okay?" Laura asked, already having read the answer on my face.

"I don't know. I can't believe I am in this mess."

"Are you ready to talk a little more about Andrew and your marriage?"

"Andrew came into my life when I wasn't ready for a relationship, but I couldn't deny how his attention transformed how I saw myself. He made me laugh. Once, he was doing his imitation of Alfalfa from *Little Rascals*, he made me snurf my wine—you know, when what you are drinking comes out your nose. Laughing is very underrated. Gosh, he was funny." I sighed in recollection. "He made me feel things I didn't know I could. For the first time in my life, I wasn't thought of as insignificant or dumb. Someone was finally seeing me. The real me. Boy, I was a smitten kitten."

She giggled at my phraseology. "What was his home life like?"

"I guess normal-ish—a lot of testosterone."

I continued to relay my memories to Laura the best I could, hopeful sharing would somehow help me make sense of the mess I was in.

Andrew is the eldest of six boys. He always talked about the old Italian neighborhood where he grew up. A place where cousins lived next door and grandparents lived across the street. Everyone in the neighborhood was family.

He both loved and feared his father, Vito, who worked hard at the Port Elizabeth docks. His job was not glamorous, but it paid the bills. His hands were calloused, his humor rough, and he was always quick to grab the belt. He's the type of person who cheers when contestants land on 'BANKRUPT' on the *Wheel of Fortune*. His mother, Anna, is a sweet, soft-spoken angel who'd moved to America from Lucca, Italy, before she met Andrew's father. She kept their small three-bedroom Cape Cod house immaculate and ensured all her men were clean and well-fed, which was a full-time job unto itself. Her days were filled with laundry, chores, and lots of noise, but she loved it. Her boys were her life.

Andrew and his mom had an incredibly close relationship. Since he was the eldest, he was second in command. He took on many of the responsibilities his mother didn't have time to finish. He aided in washing and feeding his five brothers. He was a world-class ironer and still managed to have straight A's in school. He didn't have many friends. There was never enough time.

His brother, Vinny, needed help with his homework daily. Vinny was gorgeous, but academically, everything was a little more challenging. Andrew told me how his mother would still speak in Italian. "That poor boy, bel niente. He is beautiful, but God didn't give him much up here," she would whisper while tapping at her temple.

His mother wears her hair in a twist at the back of her head, secured with a wooden spoon, just like you see in the movies. If you ask one of the boys, they will say she kept it there for easy access for when they misbehaved. She always had on an apron caked with gravy and dark purple circles under her eyes. Poor thing, she worked so hard.

Andrew understood his family depended on him, and his father had extremely high expectations. Andrew would never let him down—or any of them, for that matter. He lived in constant fear of not being good enough. No matter how hard he tried, he would never win his father's approval, and he was right.

His only escape would be college. Andrew told me how late one night, he waited for his father to return home. "Papa, I sent in my college applications today," Andrew told him excitedly.

"Bene," his father shook his head in approval. "You better get into a good one. I don't bust my ass all day so you can work the docks like me."

"I know, Papa. I'm trying really hard. You'll see; I'm gonna make you proud."

"Yeah, we'll see. Go check on your brothers and get to bed," his father ordered without glancing in his way.

"Okay, Papa," he said quietly and slinked off as instructed. He was glad his father wasn't looking at him, so the sadness in his eyes wasn't obvious.

When I'm at their house, I can see how Vito's attention goes to the others. The ones that were more like him, not the one who needed him most.

It was with some relief when Andrew set off for Boston University after high school on a full academic scholarship. The day he left, Vito wasn't home to see him off. According to Andrew, it was his mother and brothers who waved goodbye from the brick front stoop of their little house.

"Andrew, you be a good boy now," Anna held him with tear-filled eyes.

"Don't worry, Mama. I'm going to be fine; I promise." He wiped away the tears running down her cheek.

"You're my angel boy. I'm so proud of you. Study hard." With each word, her voice cracked with emotion. "O mio caro, I am going to miss you so."

"I'll miss you too," he said, wrapping his arms around her and picking her up off her feet. They all laughed.

"Get outta here, Mr. Brainiac, and get yourself one of those fancy college educations," bellowed his brother Christopher.

"Yeah, get outta here," chimed in his baby brother, Stephen. "Don't forget about us little peons stuck in dirty Jersey!"

"Guys, you better help Mama out. If you don't, I'll come home and kick your collective asses, you understand?" Andrew called over his shoulder as he walked toward his rusty blue Chevy Chevelle.

He loaded his suitcases, homemade pignoli cookies, and the container of sausage and peppers his mother had packed for the ride. He waved goodbye with a plastic fork stuck between his teeth.

While in college, Andrew continued his pursuit of academic excellence and learned a little about life along the way. It was when he met his first real girlfriend, Jenna, to whom he lost his virginity. He had his first hangover from a night of Captain Morgan's rum and made some friendships that would last a lifetime.

Shortly after graduation, he returned to his home. He went to work as a Junior Accountant at one of the most prestigious firms in New York City. His analytic brain was equal to the task. He followed the path set out before him with no need to veer. There was no room for error or emotional decisions in Andrew's life. He wanted order and predictability, or so he thought, until he met me.

Chapter 16

IT WAS A DREARY Saturday afternoon. Andrew was playing golf, and I was home with nothing to do. I found myself in his office again, staring at the blank computer screen. Did I dare look? Who was I kidding? Of course, I would.

First, I checked the bookmarks, and they were gone. The history showed nothing but the usual sports scores and news topics. I sat back in his chair with a sigh of relief and a smile. Right before I shut down, I impulsively checked the deleted files, and there they were. The date and time stamps showed he was logging on after I went to sleep. He hadn't stopped. He had just found a better way to hide it.

That night when we went to bed, I reached over and kissed him to gauge his reaction. He kissed me back. I ran my fingers lightly down his spine with one hand and caressed his sleeping member with the other. "Honey, do you mind if we wait until morning? I'm tired." He rolled over, took my arm, and wrapped it around him. I lay quietly thinking, 'I'd be tired too if I were up all night jerking off.'

When he thought I was asleep, he lifted the covers. Slowly, the mattress on his side of the bed started to rise with the absence of his body weight. The old wood floors creaked as he made his way down the hall to his office. Within moments, the flickering lights of the computer screen bounced off the otherwise dark room. I could hear the muffled sounds of his self-gratification. He was gone no longer than fifteen minutes. When he returned, I did not show that I had uncovered what was happening.

His nightly excursions had become a ritual. I kept my silence, watching each night from the loneliness of our bed. I didn't tell anyone what was happening. I was ashamed that I had failed him.

He was slipping away, leaving only the ghost of who he was. The intimacy I had been longing for was expended in a world where I was excluded. I had no way to compete with flashing pictures of human perfection, accompanied by the beautiful silence he craved. Later that night, Andrew found me sitting on the floor in his dark office.

"What are you doing? Come back to bed," he called from the door while yawning.

I tried to speak through the tears caught in my throat. "Why don't you make love to me anymore? What are you getting here that I can't give you?" I cried. "What is wrong with me? I love you so much that I can't breathe. Why are you doing this?"

"I'm so sorry, Honey. I know you don't believe me, but I do love you. Please come back to bed. Let me hold you."

"No. I'm not going anywhere. I want an explanation."

"I don't have one." He left the room with his head hung low, leaving me on the floor in anguish.

When my tears dried, all that was left was rage. I walked down the hall, where he was sound asleep. He had turned himself off just like a machine. His snoring triggered something primal in me. I pulled my arm back, closed my hand into a fist, and punched him in the head. I jumped up and straddled his body, continuing to swing wildly as I yelled, "How could you ruin my life? How dare you! You are no different from the rest of them. You are a sick sadistic fuck!" He flipped me over, pinning my hands to my side. I felt helpless underneath him. At that moment, I hated him. I cursed the day I ever met him. "Get the fuck off of me! Don't you ever hold me down, you motherfucker!" His hands were still tight around my wrists. "I said, get the fuck off!" With all the strength I could muster, I threw him to the floor. No one would ever pin me down again.

Andrew sat stunned by what had happened. Exhausted and sad, I leaned against the wall and crumpled to the ground.

"I'm so sorry, Jul. I keep fucking up. I don't know why. I wish I did. I love you. I swear on my life. Please give me another chance. I never wanted to hurt you. Please, Baby."

Slowly, he approached me, extending his hands to help me up. His cheeks were wet with tears. He had never cried in front of me before. He hardly showed any emotion of any kind. I wrapped my arms around him, and he carried me to bed.

We were both struggling against something that we didn't understand. It was destroying us.

Everything seemed to change after that night. Andrew started to come home earlier, and we began to grow close once again. He would not only go to bed with me, but he would stay with me. The comfort and the heat of his body warmed me throughout the night.

Chapter 17

FOUR MONTHS LATER, I impatiently waited for Andrew to leave for work. Once he was gone, I went into the bathroom to open the cardboard box hidden beneath the towels. After following the instructions, I waited for the liquid to flow into the result screen. One line appeared, confirming I did the test correctly, then a second, darker line showed up in the tiny plastic window.

Hardly able to keep myself from calling Andrew, my mother, sister, or shouting my news from the rooftops, I ran to the bookstore and bought half a dozen books on the subject.

Somehow, a tiny little baby was growing inside of me—evidence that our love was real.

Andrew came home to find a jar of strained peas, mashed beef, and a baby bottle filled with milk in the place where his dinner should have been. When he turned to me with confusion, I motioned to the stack of books on the counter.

Finally, a look of comprehension crossed his face. "Are you sure?"

"I'm very sure." I pulled the pregnancy test stick out of my back pocket to show him. His face lit up as he gave a celebratory hoot. "I told you I was going to make everything okay," he said, twirling me through the air. "I'm gonna be a daddy."

As the months passed, our earlier problems were conveniently forgotten. Our lives revolved around the development of our child. Our evenings were spent reading poetry and Shakespeare aloud while we listened to classical music. We ate ice cream at two in the morning, then stayed awake to feel the baby react to the sugar, watching my stomach ripple with movement.

"Oh, did you see that one?"

"Holy cow! Was that a foot or an elbow?

"A foot." My face twisted in discomfort.

"How do you know?"

"Because its elbow is firmly in my rib cage," I groaned.

I wasn't complaining. I loved every minute. Our baby was going to have a perfect life. I would make sure of it.

One afternoon, while out shopping, I received an urgent call from Andrew. "Jul, you're not going to believe this, but there is a leak in the bathroom, and everything is getting wet. Could you come home and help?"

I was unsure what he wanted an eight-month pregnant woman to do, but I obliged and hurried home. As I walked up the cement stairs, my feet rebelled against the shoes containing their ever-expanding girth. I opened the door with one final exhausted huff and was startled by the cheer of "SURPRISE!"

The house was filled with pink and blue balloons, and all of our family and friends. In the corner sat a beautiful crib filled with gifts covered in various pastel wrappings. Andrew stood on the stairs, looking down at me. "Surprise," he said with a smile. "

I mouthed the words "thank you" as the sea of guests engulfed me.

Our bundle of joy didn't seem to want to make its grand entrance. Ten and a half months, and our baby was still inside. I was beginning to think that I would be the first woman to stay pregnant forever.

I tried every wives' tale I could find: Chinese food and sex, cod liver oil with orange juice, deep knee bends, nipple stimulation for hours. As enjoyable as the last one sounds, it lost its luster after about ten minutes. Unfortunately, nothing worked. The baby needed to come out soon, or I was going to explode.

On my next appointment with the doctor, I waddled my way into the examination room. "We will perform a couple of tests on the baby to ensure it is still doing okay. Just lay back and relax," my doctor said.

"Okay. Make sure my baby is fine, and then, please, I beg of you, have mercy, and make it come out."

"Okay, okay," she said, unable to hide her smile.

They placed an elastic belt around my engorged belly and recorded the baby's every movement and beat of its heart. We all gawked as a strip of paper was expelled from the machine. After thirty minutes, it was turned off. "The baby's heart is strong but showing signs of slight distress. It's nothing to worry about, but I think it's time to move things along."

"But is my baby going to be okay?" I was panic stricken.

"Yes, the baby is fine." I searched her face for any telltale signs that this was worse than she said, but couldn't find one.

"We will send you to the hospital now, and they will begin your induction. Don't worry; everything is going to be all right. By tomorrow, you will have your baby." She wiped the jelly off my protruding and helped me off the table.

I called Andrew from the doctor's office to tell him the news. He was on the next train home. Ninety minutes later, he showed up in the admissions office, disheveled and out of breath, with the suitcase that had been packed for two months.

As they led us to our room, we held hands, giddy with anticipation. I changed into the highly accessible blue and white hospital gown and climbed into bed.

I was ready to have my baby.

The hours passed, and nothing happened. The excitement was beginning to wane. We had no idea labor would take so long. The contractions started but were mild and far apart. After four hours, I was only a centimeter dilated.

"Julianne, it could be another eight or nine hours before you're ready," Dr. Percy informed us after another examination. "Why don't you both get some rest, and I'll be back in the morning."

"The morning? Is she crazy? Do you think it will take that long?" I hoped Andrew might say something to comfort me.

"What do I know? If that's what she thinks, I'm going home to sleep in our bed. This chair sucks." He stretched out his back with a moan. "If you need me, I'll come right back. Okay?"

"I do need you. Please stay. I don't want to be alone. Here, you can lie in bed with me."

"There's hardly enough room for you." He laughed. "Come on; everything will be fine. I'll be a bigger help when you need me if I'm well rested." I don't know if he was trying to convince himself or me.

I didn't argue. He had a way of making me believe that he was always right, and I was just a silly little girl.

I spent hours watching my baby's heartbeat. It was comforting to know that I wasn't alone. I had the child inside me that I loved with all my heart. Listening to the strong and steady beats began to lull me to sleep. My eyes grew heavy and closed for a moment, and as they did, an alarm screeched next to my bed. In terror, my eyes shot open just in time to watch the count of the heartbeat drop drastically. The nurse ran in to check the tape shooting out of the machine. I saw panic in her face before she was able to mask it with her years of training. Within a moment, the heart rate climbed back up and eventually leveled off to a normal rhythm.

The nurse turned to me and said, "Don't worry, honey. The baby is tired. It is perfectly normal in a pregnancy that has gone as long as yours. I'll tell the on-call doctor, but honestly, there's nothing for you to worry about." She patted my hand in reassurance. "Go ahead and get some rest. You're going to need all your strength for tomorrow."

How was I going to sleep? I wouldn't take my eyes off the monitor again until the doctor arrived in the morning at five. After a complete examination, Dr. Percy determined that the baby needed extra prompting to come out. An intravenous drip of Pitocin was placed in my arm to speed the contractions. When that didn't work, she announced her intention to rupture the amniotic sac manually.

An apparatus not unlike a knitting needle was removed from a hermetically sealed package and inserted into my vagina. I closed my eyes tightly, not wanting to watch as it painfully explored my uterus.

After several minutes, "I'm sorry, Julianne, it won't rupture. We're going to have to perform a cesarean section."

I called Andrew right after the doctor confirmed the next step. "Please hurry up and get here. God, I'm nervous. I can't believe it is going to happen." My hand shook as I held the receiver.

"I'll leave in ten minutes. Don't be nervous; everything is going to be fine. See you in a few." I heard the click of the receiver and imagined him running around the house in a rush to get to me.

My daydreams about the arrival of the baby were growing more vivid. I could almost feel its weight in my arms. I reveled in the spirituality of the moment but was brought back to reality by the fetal monitor alarm. The doctor and the nurse returned immediately, but the heartbeat quickly started climbing back up within seconds. I wasn't sure how much longer I would be able to handle the emotional roller coaster. The constant extremes of euphoria and terror were beginning to take their toll.

Dr. Percy sat on the edge of my bed and said in a soothing voice, "The baby is going to be fine. Trust me. You must have taken excellent care of this baby for it not to want to come out." Hearing that made me smile and alleviated some of my tension. I had taken good care of my baby and always would.

Hours passed, and Andrew was nowhere to be found. The anesthesiologist arrived for the spinal block. As the needle pressed against my spine, a warmth spread through the lower half of my body, numbing all sensation.

The orderlies rolled me down the antiseptic hall on the transportation gurney; I watched as the fluorescent light flickered. Once inside the operating room, my brain went as numb as my body. At the table stood seven people, masked and gowned, who awaited my arrival. Once transferred, they removed my gown. Any modesty I may have had in the past vanished at that moment.

"Julianne, we're going to have to begin. We can't wait for Andrew any longer; your baby has to come out now." Dr. Percy smiled at me sympathetically.

"I know. It's okay. Let's have a baby." I tried to sound upbeat.

As the last word came out, Andrew walked in wearing full surgical scrubs. "Sorry, everyone. I didn't mean to keep you waiting. Time flies when you're online," he chuckled.

I did my best not to cry. I didn't want my child to see me in tears the first time we met.

The procedure began without fanfare. I could hear instruments rattle as they were thrown back down on the awaiting tray. The doctors and nurses spoke in shorthand while tugging at my abdomen. It didn't hurt; however, it was a most peculiar sensation. As I was jostled around, I silently prayed.

My beautiful baby boy screamed his first newborn cry as he was lifted from my body. The nurse bundled him up and placed him on my chest. His skin was dry and cracked, hanging on him like an oversized suit. "Is he okay?" I asked the nurse with deep concern.

"Your son is fine. Sometimes the placenta can fail, and the amniotic fluid seeps out, explaining why the doctor could not rupture the sac. It's been a while since he has had a decent meal. Once he starts nursing, he will plump up quickly, I promise."

I took in every inch of his perfect face, his intricate ears, and his pursed lips, looking for something to suck on. I was madly, passionately, and completely in love. A love so intense that words could not do it justice.

Two days later, it was time to leave the hospital. We were eager to introduce Jack to the blue and yellow nursery I had spent months obsessing over. The bedding had already been washed and waited for him in his crib. His clothes were in his drawers. The diapers, creams, powder sat on a changing table, and a glider was in the corner, where I planned to rock away the hours.

Our dream child was coming home. The one that would deliver our marriage to a place of love and security, erasing the past.

Chapter 18

HOW I WISH SOMEONE had invented a handbook on life. I was so tired of learning everything the hard way. *What to Expect, When You're Expecting* did not warn me how difficult it would be to come home with a new baby. If it did, I completely missed that chapter. The television that raised me was filled with misinformation. The Gerber Baby is a myth.

I was utterly unprepared for the world I had entered. Perhaps I was naïve, but my visions of motherhood included lazily rocking in the nursery, with my precious angel at my breast. I imagined Andrew in the background, doing laundry, and making dinner. The reality of the situation was entirely different. In fact, it sucked.

My life was now all about feeding on demand. Within the first few days, my nipples were raw and cracked. Every suck delivered excruciating jolts radiating through my body. I was ready to give up, but Andrew wouldn't allow it.

"Come on, you can do this," he cheered me along. "Remember what the books say; you're making him strong and healthy."

"I know, Andrew, but it hurts! You have no idea!" I shrieked in pain.

"You can do this. How will you feel if he gets sick, knowing you might have been able to prevent it?"

He was playing dirty, but he was right. "I'll do it for him," I grimaced with each suck.

When Jack wasn't nursing, he was crying; when he was nursing, I was crying. After a month, I no longer could tell the difference between day and night. Time was wholly lost to me.

I read all the infant books, trying to figure out why Jack wasn't sleeping and why no amount of comfort could soothe him. Was he sick? Was it colic? I didn't even know what colic was. The only thing I did know was that something had to be wrong. I was at my wit's end, so we went to visit the pediatrician's office, hoping they would be able to tell me what to do.

I walked into the office, and the gray-haired woman slid open the glass partition. "Do you have an appointment?"

"No, but I really need to see the doctor. Something is wrong with my baby." Once again, I was on the verge of tears.

"I'm sorry, dear, but you must have an appointment. If it's an emergency, you can go to the hospital; otherwise, we can see him tomorrow." She looked down at the black book in front of her. "Hmm, I have a 10 o'clock open. Would that work for you?"

"No, I don't think so." My face burned with anger. "We'll wait right here until someone is available."

She rolled her eyes while closing the sliding glass window. I could not ascertain what she said to the other staff, but I didn't care. I wasn't going anywhere. Pacing back and forth in the waiting room, I purposely passed the receptionist's window so everyone in the office could bear witness to my son's pain.

"Ma'am, you are going to have to find a way to settle him down," one of the nurses said, peeking through the door. "We can't hear ourselves think."

"What would you suggest?" I snapped at her.

She looked around the waiting room where no one else was present; we were ushered into an exam room by a nurse. "Let's put you into room three and take a look." Finally, someone was showing me sympathy.

"Thank you so much."

The diagnosis was colic. There was no cure or secret remedy. We would have to wait for him to outgrow it, and the doctors said there was no way of knowing when that would be. I was sent away with some advice and a tightness in my chest.

That evening when Andrew walked in the door, I handed Jack to him.

"Take him. I have to go outside. I can't take it another minute."

Before he had a chance to reply, I stepped into the cold night air to remove the screaming that never stopped playing in my head. While on the front porch, I could still hear Jack's torment. His cries were growing louder and more severe by the minute. Glancing in the window, I could see Jack strapped into the infant seat with his back arching, face red, and gasping between cries. Andrew sat inches away, oblivious, watching the Yankees.

Yanking the door open, I screamed in frustration, "Get up and walk around with him or rock him! He's so uncomfortable. He needs to be held."

"No, Jul. You see, that's the problem. You're spoiling him. He needs to learn how to soothe himself. Hey, it's a brutal world out there. My father didn't rock me."

"That may explain why you're such an asshole!" I said, leaning down to pick up Jack.

My son and I spent the first six months of his life crying and taking comfort in each other's arms. I learned to function on the little sleep I could catch while rocking him. I didn't resent having to give up the luxuries of sleep and food; I only wanted to have someone to commiserate with.

Andrew was back to coming home late and locking himself in his office. We passed each other in the hallway, mere visitors in each other's lives.

If I were to be completely honest, I liked it better when he wasn't home. Looking at him made my blood boil, and hearing his voice made me cringe. Many times, I found myself praying he wouldn't come home at all. That wish was almost granted on September 11th, 2001.

Jack and I went on our usual hour's morning stroll, returning home shortly before nine o'clock. While he sat in his highchair eating Cheerios, I read from his favorite book, *Brown Bear, Brown Bear What Do You See?*

The first phone call that came in was from Sarah. "Jul, can you believe what is happening?"

"What are you talking about?" I asked, annoyed that she was interrupting our morning ritual.

"Is your television on?"

"No. I'm feeding Jack. Something wrong? Where are you?"

"I'm upstate. Don't worry about that; turn on the TV now!" she yelled.

"What channel?"

"Any channel. It's everywhere." I couldn't tell if she was panicking or laughing. "Where's Andrew?" She demanded to know.

"At work, thank God. Wait a second; I'm turning it on now." I gasped as I watched smoke billowing out of one of the World Trade Center towers. "What the hell is going on?" I shrieked in horror.

"A plane hit it. They still don't know what happened." Sarah's voice couldn't hide the terror she felt.

As she spoke, I tried to listen to what Katie Couric was saying. Suddenly, I heard a beep indicating I had another call.

"Got to go, Sarah. It might be Andrew. I'll call you back."

"Hello?" My voice was tentative.

"Hey, it's me. Are you watching the news?" His voice was oddly calm.

"Yes, what's going on?"

"They aren't telling us anything yet."

"Can you see it from your building?"

"Oh yeah, it's right outside my window. It's unbelievable. People are jumping from the Trade Center." He spoke as if he was detached from the events surrounding him.

"Get out of there, Andrew. You need to come home!"

"I can't. We have been told to stay put. They think a plane may have lost its navigation system and crashed into the building."

"Whatever happened, we'll find out later. Please come home. I'm scared."

"I can't just leave. This is my job. I'll call you back when I have more information," he said and hung up.

When the second World Trade Center was engulfed in flames, I phoned Andrew again.

"Get the hell out of there now! Don't argue—just get out. Do you hear me, Andrew Peter Russo?" I was almost screaming.

"Yes, I'm leaving now. I'll call as soon as I can."

Moments later, the first building fell. "I can't believe this is happening," I said aloud. "Things like this don't happen here. This is crazy." I sat cross-legged on the floor, holding my son as if he would be marred by the horror I was witnessing.

The barrage of phone calls began. The next one was Andrew's mother.

"Dio Mio. I just hung up with Andrew. I can't believe this." His mother said with a thickness in her voice.

"What? He was supposed to leave 10 minutes ago. Are you sure you just spoke to him? Think, how long ago was it?"

"Non lo so."

"English, Mama." I tried to keep my voice calm.

"I don't know." She was getting flustered. "I thought it was a few minutes ago. Maybe it was more." Her voice gave me the feeling she was about to fall apart. Terror was ripping through my body. If he had just left, there was a chance he would have been caught in the flaming debris. He could be dead or dying, and I had no way of knowing.

I took a deep breath, trying to contain my fear. "It's okay, Mom. He is going to be fine. Sit tight. I will call you when I hear something." I didn't believe a word of what I was saying.

After a while, I stopped answering the phone. Everyone wanted to find out how Andrew was, and I didn't have an answer for them. I could only do what the rest of the world was doing, watch the news as it repeatedly played out the morning's tragedy and pray he would make it out safely.

As usual, Jack was my comfort. I held him in my arms as he nuzzled his sweet round head into my neck. His warmth brought me back to the stark reality that Andrew might not be coming home. People were dying—thousands of them.

It was time for me to figure out what I would do if he were gone. I went into survival mode. I figured first, I would need to sell the house. I would move somewhere near Sarah. I needed to remember where he stored the insurance policies and his will. Perhaps it seemed morbid to have such thoughts, but it was the only thing I could think to do.

One by one, most of our neighbors came home. Almost everyone was accounted for, except for my husband. The phone rang again.

"Hello. Is this Julianne Russo, Andrew Russo's wife?" an unfamiliar female voice inquired. I fell to the ground; I was sure she was going to tell me he was dead.

"It's okay," I heard the voice trying to calm me down. "He's fine. Andrew is with my husband, Richard. They are in New Jersey and on their way home. He is okay!"

"Oh my God! Thank you so much! He's alive. Thank you!" The words came out between sobs.

Not everyone was going to be that lucky. In a brief moment, we almost lost everything. Our fight seemed so petty after what had just happened.

Within an hour, he came walking up the driveway covered in black soot. Overjoyed at the sight of him, I threw the door open and ran to him with Jack on my hip. Wrapping my free arm around his neck, a sense of relief rushed over me as I felt his heart beating strongly in his chest.

"Thank God, Baby. I was so scared. I never want to lose you. I love you so much."

"Stop it, Julie," he said, pushing me away. "You're making a scene. Let's go inside. I'm hungry, and it's been a bitch of a day."

Chapter 19

THE COLIC THAT HAD permeated my life for almost 365 days, without time off for good behavior, was finally over. Jack was on his way to becoming a happy, fun, and loving toddler.

We had made it through the first year. I say we, meaning Jack and me. I was finally getting some sleep and had a sense of peace about my place in the world. I was Jack's mother, which was the most important job I could ever hold and all I needed. Our love for each other gave me the strength to go after what was once mine.

Andrew and I no longer had anything that resembled a normal relationship. Osama bin Laden's henchmen stole the last trace of the man I had once known.

One day, as Jack napped, I logged onto Andrew's computer and scrolled through the history. He was visiting the pornographic sites in the morning, evening, and middle of the night. On weekends when I was running errands, and he was supposed to be watching Jack, he was there. He was no longer a visitor in the digital world. It had become his home. The females he took to bed didn't have crying babies, leaking breasts, or dark circles under their eyes. They didn't care what time he came home at night, and nothing he said made them cry or fly into a hormonal frenzy.

In the world he created, he had total control over everyone and everything. From what I saw, he no longer had room for us. My options were the same ones I had been faced with before: stay, or go. I left a note taped to the computer monitor.

Andrew:

You have been living in a world I cannot enter. The time has come for us both to decide what we want. I will be in touch.

I love you, but I don't know if I can keep holding on.

Julie

Buckling Jack into his car seat, I said, "Don't worry, sweetheart, Mommy will always do what's best for you, even if she's not sure what that is." I bent over and kissed him on the forehead. He looked up at me with those soulful brown eyes and that smile that melted my heart. "I love you!" I said, before shutting the door.

As I pulled away, tears rolled down my face. I wasn't sure why I was crying. I wasn't sad or even angry. Oddly, I didn't feel much of anything at all.

Unsure of where I was going, I headed out of town. After three hours of driving, I found a bed-and-breakfast in Cape May, New Jersey, with a small carriage house for rent. We had found a temporary home.

It was as if the place had been waiting for us. Everything felt familiar and comfortable. The interior of the cottage was painted in shades of blue and green. The furniture was white wicker that had been painted at least a dozen times over the years, and baskets of seashells from previous tenants sat atop the tables.

Jack and I spent six days making castles in the sand and looking for shells to leave behind for the next occupants to enjoy. During our week's stay, I realized that I was perfectly capable of raising my son on my own. I didn't need Andrew, but I did need his money. If we ran away, eventually I would have to get a job. While contemplating our next move, I looked on as my baby slept. He was curled in a ball, knees tucked under his chest, with his sweet little tush in the air. Every breath I took was in rhythm with his. The sight of him, so content, filled me with love. "Oh, my baby, I wish I knew what to do," I whispered.

The mere thought of leaving him with strangers in daycare tore at my heart. How would I be able to protect him if I wasn't there? He would be at the mercy of his caregiver, and I could never allow that.

The next afternoon, we pulled up to our house. Andrew was sitting on the porch swing with a beer in hand. It was almost as if he knew we were coming.

"Hey," I yelled up at him as I stepped out of the car.

He slowly stood and leaned over the rail closest to me. "Are you home, or did you come back to pack the rest of your things?"

"We're home. Jack needs to be here."

"What about you? What do you need?"

"Just my son and a husband, if I can find one around here." I craned my neck to look around in every direction.

"You already have both." He came down the stairs, hugged me, and whispered, "I missed you."

I didn't say I missed him too because I hadn't.

Chapter 20

ANOTHER YEAR PASSED, AND we, as a family, fell into a groove that was tolerable. I joined Mommy and Me gym classes with Jack and a local women's book club in the hopes of expanding my life and finding some joy. Perhaps we were living in a state of denial, but at least it was peaceful. I no longer demanded answers or threatened to leave, and he no longer worked late.

Jack, the center of my universe, was turning two. I began to long for another child. I still had so much love to give.

One night, when Jack was fast asleep, and Andrew was in his office, and I put on a black lace teddy that had been hanging on a hook in my closet for so long I had to blow off the dust. I fixed my hair, put on a little makeup, and started the seduction.

"What are you doing?" Andrew leaned back in the chair with his eyes bulging.

"What does it look like?" I began to nibble at his ear.

"I believe you're trying to seduce me, Mrs. Robinson." He said in his best Dustin Hoffman voice.

The laughter that exploded out of me may not have been romantic, but it gave me hope that the Andrew I once loved was somewhere inside. Once my laughter subsided, and his ego was adequately inflated, I went into action. The following month, two new lines appeared in the plastic window.

My pregnancy brought Andrew and me together as it did when I was pregnant with Jack. We gave our unborn child the same care, love, and attention. Again, I was blessed with caring for something beyond intrinsic value.

Five weeks into my pregnancy, while leaning over the kitchen sink washing the morning's dishes, my back began to ache terribly. What started as minor discomfort grew to such pain, I dropped to my knees and doubled over on the cold tile floor. Wrapping my arms around my stomach and I rocked, trying to keep the pain at bay. A warm, thick, dark liquid began seeping through my jeans and clung to my legs. Slowly, I stood upright, holding the counter for balance, and made my way to the bathroom.

As I sat, my body released a red spherical object that could only have been one thing: my baby. The very thought made me vomit on my feet. When the worst of it had passed, I placed a maxi pad between my legs. I carefully drove myself to the doctor's office, reminding myself along the way that I still had one baby to protect riding in the back.

Upon examination, the doctor confirmed my suspicions. The only thing that would remain of my pregnancy would be the empty place in my heart that would always be reserved for my angel in Heaven.

When I arrived back home, I let Jack watch *The Electric Company* as I nursed myself. I told Andrew later that night after we put Jack to bed. He was sweet and held me until I fell asleep.

The following day, the sun came up just like always. No amount of grief could stop the dawning of a new day. I sat in my bed, mourning the loss of my child. Andrew came in and held my hand tenderly. He kissed the top of my head and said, "I'll be home around seven. Give me a call if you need anything." With that, he left. It never occurred to him that what I needed was him home with me. I walked to the window. "I can't believe you're going to work," I cried while watching him drive away. "Sometimes, I hate you so much."

I swallowed four ibuprofen tablets, stuck a maxi pad to my panties, and went to take care of my son. Mommies don't get sick days.

I wondered if my miscarriage may have been God's way of saying we shouldn't have another baby—but what if I was wrong? Maybe that baby wasn't meant to be born, but another would. Was it fair of me to deny my son a sibling? Was it fair to deny myself another child to love? Four months later, I was pregnant again. I was terrified of losing this child, scared to the point of obsession. I had weekly visits with Dr. Percy, who tried to convince me the baby was healthy, which, of course, I didn't believe. I insisted on monthly sonograms to alleviate my seemingly irrational fears.

At my twenty-week appointment, I had yet another sonogram, but this time something was different. The wand they used repeatedly passed over the same area. No one said anything at first; they looked at each other as if telepathically trying to decide how much information they needed to divulge.

"Julianne, everything is looking pretty good. The baby is right on target for weight and size. We have one small concern. Do you see this shadow over here on the right temporal lobe?" she asked while pointing to a darkened area of the brain. "Uh-huh," I grunted, too scared to speak.

"There is a chance that it is a mass on the baby's brain, but before you get upset, it's not completely uncommon. They often go away on their own in four to five weeks. On the outside chance that it doesn't, it is a possible early warning of a developmental issue. You will need to come back in six weeks for a follow-up."

She should know me well enough by now to understand why I would most certainly be upset. Holy crap, when was life going to get easy?

Each week dragged endlessly. I went through the motions of playing with Jack and teaching him the alphabet. We went to the park, sang at music class, and spent each waking moment with each other. I tried to act as normal as possible.

The six weeks ended, and it was finally time for the long-awaited follow-up sonogram. I was escorted into examination room two. Jack sat in the corner with his firetruck. In walked Dr. Percy, and spotting Jack in the corner, "How are you doing, sport? Do you want to come over and see the baby?"

Jack looked at the doctor with trepidation and sidled over to the table.

We held his hand as the black-and-white image appeared on the screen.

"Okay, now here's the heart. See it beating? It's very strong. Now let's take a look at that troublesome area." She passed the wand over my stomach, trying to get a full picture.

"Nothing there. No more mass. The baby looks perfectly healthy in every respect. You can start breathing now, Julianne."

I was bursting to share the news with Andrew, knowing he would be equally relieved.

Jack and I rushed home, trying to arrive before Andrew returned from work. After pulling into the garage, we saw he was already home. Jack and I donned our detective hats and began 'Operation: Locate Big Daddy.' We slowly climbed the stairs, smiling at each other, trying not to laugh. Once at the top, we got down on the ground and crawled on our hands and knees to find our objective. Jack's face was close to the ground with a look of determination across his face. He reached the door before me and pushed it open. "You're under arrest!" Jack yelled with his fingers in the shape of a gun.

I arrived just in time to see Andrew bending over to pull up his pants. On the computer screen, two women were performing oral sex. "Jesus Christ, Andrew! I'm finding out if our baby is okay, and this is what you're doing? What the hell is wrong with you? You are so twisted." I screamed, snatching Jack up and running out of the room. Andrew came running out after us, zipping up as he went. I ran out of the house and down the street. I needed to put distance between us as quickly as possible.

Jack and I wandered around town until his eyes grew tired. I carried him home with his little head resting upon my shoulder, and his feet dangling past my hips. After putting him in his crib, I went into our bedroom without stopping to speak with Andrew. I stared at myself in the bathroom mirror, wondering how much more I could take. Andrew was standing behind me when I turned around.

"I'm sorry. I know I keep saying that, but I really am. I love you."

The door to my heart had been closed, and as much as I wished I could re-open it, I couldn't take the risk. I wouldn't ever be able to rely on him or trust him. I've never been able to rely on anyone. I should have learned that a long time ago.

With each monthly appointment, I watched my child grow healthy and strong. That was how I viewed it—*my* child.

A cesarean section was scheduled for the baby to be born at thirty-six weeks. Dr. Percy didn't want to chance another failed placenta.

Once again, they rearranged the trunk of my body to gain access to the baby. I couldn't wait. *Would Jack have a brother or a sister?* I wondered.

A tiny bloody body was lifted high into the air, looking impossibly small. "It's a girl!" the doctor said. "You have a perfect set. What's her name going to be?"

In the previous months, I thought long and hard about her name. "Tess. It's a derivative of Teresa, meaning strong. The world better watch out, cause

Tess is in town." No one was going to mess with my daughter.

My baby girl was breathing and crying. Tess Elizabeth Russo. She will be strong. She will be vibrant. She will be wise. She will be anything she wants... as long as she isn't anything like me, I thought.

Tess was whisked away by the nurse to be evaluated, cleaned, and weighed. I was incredibly blessed. I had my perfect baby girl and my amazing little boy. Things were going to start getting better. I knew they were. They had to.

From the first night Tess came home, I slept in her room under the soothing light of her illuminated mobile. The stars flicker around the room as I held my hand on her back, feeling her every breath. I wouldn't let my daughter out of my sight. Each morning Jack would come in, and the three of us would lie on an air mattress on the floor, holding each other under a blanket of love. Andrew lurked outside the door, knowing he was not welcome.

Again, I escaped into the world of motherhood. I was the overprotective and over-involved mom. We did everything as a single unit. I was tucked safely in my hiding place, watching my children grow and learn. Helping them adjust to the world gave me purpose. Days rolled by, one by one. Those days turned into months and months into years.

When I least expected it, the nightmares returned.

Chapter 21

"You've been through a lot, Julie. We have a lot of issues to tackle. I think there is still more going on. Let's start by talking about the abuse you suffered as a child," she nodded as she spoke.

Her words made me uncomfortable. My body stiffened in response. "Abuse? I'm not sure I call what happened abuse. Would you?"

"Of course, I would. You are a victim of child abuse, sexual abuse, and neglect."

"Hold on. I am not a victim of anything. I never let anyone or anything beat me down. I was... I am stronger than that." My voice grew louder than I had intended, but I would never be classified as a victim. Victims in my eyes were weak, and I wasn't weak. I had spent my life proving that.

"Ok, but we still have to look at how your past affected your life and the choices you have made. Many of your issues are a direct result of your experiences."

"You're right. That's why you're the doc. I know we need to talk about it, but can we deal with one crisis at a time? I'm having an issue that I don't know how to deal with. Andrew is downright mean to Tess."

"In what way?" she questioned.

"He has no patience for her and always yells at her. If it were Jack, he would never do that. I'm telling you, if he doesn't watch himself, we will all disappear, and he will never see any of us again."

"Why do you think he has singled out Tess?"

"I wish I knew. Maybe she reminds him of me," I guessed.

"Maybe." Laura raised her eyebrows. "It is possible his anger is at women in general. Julie, he would not be the first man with repressed feelings that come out in a misguided attempt for control."

"I know. I have thought about it, but honestly, I can't for the life of me find evidence of anything happening in his life that would reflect that. His mother is a saint. He should love women. Something else is going on."

"Have you shared what's been happening in your life with anyone?"

"I told Danni a little, but not much. Something hilarious happened the other day." I couldn't help but laugh out loud.

"Tell me."

"I told Danni we never have sex, and I'm totally frustrated. She asked if I had a vibrator."

"Well, do you?" Laura was completely unphased by the topic.

"No. Well, not until a few days ago when I found a package on my front porch. I opened it. There was an enormous flesh-tone mechanical penis. I swear, it was as if it was chopped off some poor guy's body!" I chuckled. "Danni is a riot. So now, I am the proud owner of an eight-inch battery-operated penis. I think I'll name it Fred."

"Okay," Laura said, steering the conversation back to the matter at hand. "Have you told Sarah or your mother about what is happening in your life?"

"Sarah knows a little. She thinks I should leave him. Her exact words were, 'Kick his sorry ass out and change the locks,' but she is not exactly the most pro-relationship person. After Jimmy died, she had two disastrous divorces; she thinks all men are pigs. She might be right. Anyway, she is having a hard enough time staying sober. I don't want to add any more stress to her already chaotic life."

"Can you tell me a little more about Sarah?"

"You pretty much know the nutshell of it. She and I aren't particularly close, but I love her. When she lost Jimmy, I thought she was going to die. Actually, die. That was how she ended up in rehab."

"What happened to Jimmy?" Laura asked, trying to put the pieces of my dysfunctional family together.

I begin sharing the flashback of the pivotal moment that changed the course of Sarah's life forever. Jimmy was Sarah's boyfriend. I remember when they first met, Sarah was instantly taken by him. He looked like a movie star when he pulled up to the house in his fire engine red Mustang. I actually had a crush on him. I smiled at the innocent memory.

"They both loved to party and laugh. They would stay up late sipping vodka from the bottle, and I would listen in the hallway to their moans of passion.

One night, Mom and I were woken by a pounding on the front door. When I opened it, I knew it was bad news. There stood two police officers. "Ma'am, we need you to come with us. It's about your daughter. She's alive, but there has been a terrible accident." We threw on some shoes, got in the back of the cruiser, and sat quietly, wondering how bad the news would be.

When we arrived, the street was closed off. The red stripes of the emergency vehicle lights cut through the darkness like a disco, and the smell of gasoline hung heavy in the air. In the distance, I could see Sarah sitting on the curb, wrapped in a blanket, sobbing. I broke into a sprint to reach her, the cold night air waking me fully into reality. I sat next to my sister and put my arm around her, grateful she was alive. The blood from the cut on her head stained the side of her face. Her hand was bandaged, but other than that, she appeared uninjured. Following her gaze, I saw what she did. Lying on the road were two sheets covering what appeared to be bodies and a heap of twisted, smoldering metal.

"Sarah, what happened?"

"Jul, it all happened so fast," she cried. "One minute, we were singing and playing air guitar, and the next, he was gone. Oh my God, Julie, he's gone!" The sobbing became uncontrollable again.

Mom took my place by her side, and I left her to ask the police officer what had happened. He told me Jimmy reeked of alcohol. From what they could tell, he was drunk and veered into oncoming traffic. The impact was so forceful he was ejected through the windshield, landing two hundred yards away. The woman in the other car had two children in the backseat. She died on impact, and her children had already been taken to the hospital. Sarah had refused to leave Jimmy, which is why they came to get us. Once we were finally able to coax her to come home, she was a shadow of herself.

"That is awful," Laura's voice was laced with a deep sense of empathy once I finished my memory.

"It was. As I said, it almost destroyed her. After that, it was one bad relationship after another. She is dealing with her own demons. She doesn't need to deal with mine."

"I understand. How about your mother?"

"Dear God, I would never tell my mom the details of my life, no way. As far as she knows, I'm living a fairytale existence. Telling her would elicit more drama than I might be able to handle. Besides, she knows nothing about how to have a successful relationship. It's my problem, and I'll deal with it."

"Where does your father fit into the picture these days? Do you have any relationship with him?"

"No. He is on marriage number four and lives in South Carolina with his thirty-five-year-old wife and her two children."

"Do you speak to him at all?"

"Once in a while, he might send a birthday card, but that's about the extent of it."

"What about your children? Do they have any relationship with him?"

"He isn't interested in them; truth be told, I don't want them anywhere near him. He may be an old man now, but I don't think he has mellowed with age. I won't risk exposing them to that kind of anger."

"I can understand, considering what you experienced."

"Yeah. So... I have nobody. Nobody but Danni and the children, but I don't need anyone else. I made it this far."

"Yes, you have. Let's continue talking about this next week."

"Pandora's box awaits."

Chapter 22

THE NIGHT FOLLOWING MY discussion of Sarah and Jimmy with Laura, Andrew and I were alone, sitting in a room of silence when I decided to talk about what we should do. I figured if we could work out our problems independently, I wouldn't need to go back to Laura. I liked her, but didn't want to rehash the past anymore. I just want it to go away. All I had to do was try a little harder.

I swiveled on the couch to face him. "Andrew, this has been a crappy few years for us both," I said.

He snorted, not even glancing away from the muted television that flickered with the highlights of the day's sporting events.

I grabbed the remote and turned it off. "Let's wipe the slate clean. I'm so tired of being alone. I just want to be held." I put my head on his shoulder and waited for a response. I was praying somehow, magically, I would hear the words that would erase the unkind years, and we might be able to start over. After a long pause, he spoke.

"I want that too, but I can't." He was silent for a moment and then continued. "I know I love you, but I can't pretend to feel something I don't."

"What do you mean?"

He wouldn't look me in the eye. He spoke in such a low tone that it was barely audible. "I don't want to have sex with you. I don't know why. I love you and don't want to lose you. Please, give me some more time. I'm sure I can figure this out."

He wanted to be married. He wanted the world to see us as having a normal life. He wanted everything his way, but what about me? Everything is always his way.

In the past, I had tried ignorance, crying, begging, and now forgiveness, but nothing has worked. All that was left was an ultimatum.

I stood up to show that I meant business. "You need to talk to someone. You go into therapy, or I leave and take the children with me. It's your call." The final ultimatum was given.

"Okay, I'll go," he promised. "Just don't do anything drastic."

He must have taken me seriously because he had his first appointment within forty-eight hours, and I went back to see Laura the following week.

Chapter 23

AFTER THREE WEEKS OF Andrew seeing his new therapist, Dr. Peterson, I sat him down and grilled him, knowing that something had to have been unearthed by now.

"What are you two discussing? Do you talk about me? What did you tell him? What a demanding bitch I am?"

"Stop it. You know I would never say that. We talked about stuff." He tried stonewalling me, but I didn't let him off the hook.

"Well, what do you talk about? You don't sit there for an hour staring at the wall, do you? I need to know what I'm dealing with!" Still, nothing. "This is my life, too. You are the father of my children. Are you crazy? A sociopath? Are you gay? A pedophile? What is wrong with you?"

I was unrelenting but also secretly afraid of what he would say. I knew people hid all sorts of nasty secrets, and I was sure there was one lurking in there somewhere. But sometimes, some questions should never be answered. Sometimes we need to lie, if only to protect those we love, but this time, he didn't. I really wish he had.

"Don't be ridiculous. I'm not gay, I'm not crazy, and I would never ever hurt Jack or Tess or any child. I can't believe you would say that." He was disgusted by my accusations.

"Then tell me. Make me understand."

There were at least two minutes of agonizing silence before my worst fear was thrown back at me. "When we got married, I was in love with someone else."

My mouth hung open in complete surprise. I was hoping I didn't hear him correctly. Hadn't he sworn his love to me? How was it possible? "Who?" I whispered.

"Babe, I know this sounds bad, but it's not. I mean to you, it may be, but in the long run, it's not."

"What the fuck are you talking about? You are making absolutely no sense. Start at the beginning."

He began to stammer, "The year before I met you, I had dated this girl, Paige, from my office. She sat in the cubical next to mine. We only dated for six months, but I fell in love with her. At least I thought I did. I had never felt that way about anyone before."

"Go on." I tried not to let him see my jaw tighten.

"One day, out of the blue, she broke up with me without an explanation. She spent the next two months avoiding me, and then one day, she was gone. I heard she requested a transfer and was seeing someone in a different department. I never saw her again. End of story."

"I have had past relationships, too. I don't understand how this impacts us."

"I guess I never got over her. She and I had planned a future, Jul. We talked about marriage and babies. It was more than a casual fling." He stared at the rug, unwilling to look me in the eyes.

"You never told me any of this." How could he not have told me he had thought about getting married before?

"I couldn't tell you. I didn't understand myself. I mourned the loss of her and moved on. I met you a short time later, and you blew me away, Julie. As the wedding grew closer, I found myself getting so mad at you. I couldn't be in the same room as you, but I didn't want to lose you either. Dr. Peterson thinks I shut down the part of myself that offers connection to protect myself from getting hurt again. The problem was, once that happened, I had nothing to give you. I loved you. I still love you. I wanted to, and I still want to spend my life with you. Honestly, I never meant to hurt you. This has nothing to do with you." He reached out to touch my arm.

I stood and began pacing the living room like a caged animal. My hands were buried so deeply in my hair that I could have ripped every last strand out. "Are you kidding? It has everything to do with me." I could feel the thumping of my heart in my ears.

"Julie, I want to grow old with you. Please believe me." He grabbed my hand as I passed by, but I yanked it away.

"Explain how you go from being in love with her to not being in love with her." My rage could no longer be hidden as I hissed through my teeth.

"Only part of me loved her, but part of me loved you, too."

"Listen to what you're saying. You just told me you were in love with someone else when you married me. You wished I was another woman when you gave me the stupid ring." I took off my wedding band and engagement ring and flung them at him. "Jesus Christ, Andrew, how could you have done that to me?" My body felt like it was on the verge of collapsing.

This was unequivocally the worst thing a person like me could ever hear. Infidelity, even homosexuality, might have been easier for me to handle. But marrying me under false pretenses, nothing could have prepared me for that. Our lives were built on a lie. Our children conceived from a lie. The man I was madly, passionately in love with, and pledged my life to had not been in love with me. How could I have been so naïve, so stupid? Had I been so desperate to be loved that I didn't see the warning signs? He had been one of the few people in the world I had ever trusted completely. He was the one I had let into my soul and fill my heart. All I wanted was to be loved and protected. Instead, I was screwed.

"Are you going to go back?" My voice broke between words.

"To Paige?"

"No! To the doctor, you jackass." Really, how could I have married someone so clueless?

"Do you want me to?" He answered sheepishly. "Abso-fucking-lutely."

Chapter 24

WHEN I WOKE, MY wedding band and engagement ring sat sparkling on my nightstand. He must have placed them there after I fell asleep. Picking both up, I held them at arm's length, watching them glimmer in the morning light, much as I had when I first received them. They were a symbol of our love. They represented a promise we made to each other. Throwing back the covers, I dragged myself out of bed and placed them in my jewelry box, vowing never to wear them again.

Walking through the house, I removed all the wedding pictures one by one. The one on the mantle, the shot of us kissing right after we were pronounced husband and wife, the framed invitation that hung in the hallway. I took down any picture of the two of us looking as if we were the perfect happy couple. I boxed them up and put them in the basement. They were all lies.

After dropping the children at preschool, I made my way to Laura's office. I sat in the parking lot, not wanting to go in. How could I tell anyone what he said? Even Laura. But this was the answer she had been looking for, wasn't it?

I knocked lightly on the door, almost wishing she wouldn't hear me, but she asked me to come in.

"Hi. I haven't heard from you in a few weeks. How are things going?"

"Not great." I sunk down on the familiar chair. "Andrew told me all sorts of things." I filled her in on the details, allowing for all the hostility I felt to attach to each word.

"How did that make you feel?"

"Awful! How else would it make me feel? He is a liar. He's a fake, Laura! God, I am so tired of hurting all the time. I just want it to stop."

"How long have you been hurting?"

"As long as I can remember." I grabbed a tissue from the glass table beside me. "When I was a little girl, I used to pray God would take me away. When I was a teenager, I would go to the cliffs up on the Palisades and stare over the edge, wondering if anyone would be upset if I jumped. What would I be thinking about as I sailed through the air? Would I die before hitting the ground, or would I smash against the rocks, knowing my bones were splintering and my brain was seeping out?"

"Do you still want to die?"

"No, I can't. I have Jack and Tess now. I would never leave them or cause them that kind of pain intentionally. They are the only thing I have to hold on to. They are my everything."

"What if you didn't have them? Then what?"

"In that case, I probably would want to die. I would never kill myself. I think that would be completely unfair to the people I left behind. The constant pain is so hard to bear." I cradled my head in my hands and rocked back and forth. "I sometimes fantasize about slitting my wrists longways, the way they say. Maybe downing a bottle of sleeping pills with a vodka chaser. Even slicing open my chest and removing my heart to stop the pain. I know it sounds morbid, but it is nothing I would actually do."

"I know. How do you handle the pain now?"

"I don't. I have gotten good at blocking it out and pretending to be happy. I do it so well sometimes I fool myself."

"Have you ever been happy?" she asked.

There's that question again.

"I think maybe I have, a few times," I said, picturing my children.

"Tell me."

"Well, anytime my children smile. I think that's a given. When they're happy, I am happy." I smile, just thinking of them. "If we are excluding the obvious, I would have to say, when I first dated Andrew. With him, I had a clean slate. I may have mentioned this before, but he is extremely intelligent, and when I met him, he thought I was smart. Someone of his caliber thought I was bright. I had been told all my life that my strongest attribute was my body, and finding out it wasn't made me so very happy.

"I'm happy any time someone tells me they love me. But I'm also equally terrified because the odds are strong that any happiness will be ripped away. Kind of like now. I guess that doesn't count, huh?"

"That counts. Think about some other times, and we will discuss them next week. We need to find you something positive to work toward."

Chapter 25

ANDREW RECITED CHAPTER AND verse of his latest session with his therapist. After a month, they began to make headway. He started with his withdrawal from our relationship.

"When we were in the jewelry store buying the engagement ring, I thought that if I bought it and we got engaged, everything would be fine. But while we waited for it to be sized, I began to feel horribly guilty. You were so happy. It was as if you had swallowed the sun and were radiant. At that moment, I knew I didn't love you the same way."

"Then why did you do it? I didn't ask you to marry me. I didn't give any ultimatums. It was all your idea."

"As I said, I thought things would change, but they didn't. That's when I began working late and volunteering to go on business trips. If I weren't home, I wouldn't have to see the look in your eyes that I see now. I never meant to hurt you. I know I was selfish. I didn't want you to go, but I didn't want you to stay either. It doesn't make any sense, does it? I loved you, but I resented you, too. I didn't know what to do."

I sat listening, trying to be open-minded.

"All right, what about the porn?" None of what he was saying made any sense to me.

"I've always looked at porn. All guys do. I know it got out of hand, but it's much easier than having sex with you. I don't have to think about what you want, and I don't have to worry about doing it right. I can do what I want when I want."

"Don't you find pleasure in arousing someone else?" I asked.

"Not really. The doctor says this whole thing turned into an issue of control. The more I went to those sites, the better I felt. It became my escape, like you going to yoga."

"Hardly," I replied snidely. "Besides, I fucking hate yoga."

Andrew agreed to continue his visits with Dr. Peterson, but I did insist he move into the guestroom while we worked through it. I didn't have any love left for him, and I certainly had none for myself. My heart was numb. The kids and I moved into our king-sized bed, where their presence reminded me that I had a reason to get out of bed.

Back at Laura's office, I went with a new bag of crap to unload. We talked about Andrew's session and what was uncovered that week.

"Apparently, he needs to get away from me. Supposedly, that is what the whole porn thing is about. Let me ask you, if he didn't want to be with me, then why the hell did he marry me?"

"You are going to have to ask him that," she pointed at me.

"I did, but his reason sucked!" I groaned and sunk down further into the chair.

"Let's discuss why you married him."

"Because I loved him so much, I couldn't see straight. I loved him because he made me happy, laugh, and safe. I wanted to do the same for him."

"What about sex? Did you love your sex life?"

Boy, she wasn't pulling any punches. "Yes, we had a very healthy sex life at first," I said, "but then it evaporated," trying to think about if what I was saying was true.

"Let's think about how your current sexual relationship is affected by your past sexual experiences."

"No. I'm not going there," I said, putting up my hands as if pushing the memories away. "This is not about me; it's about him. He is the one who stopped having sex with me. He's the one with the problem. I didn't instigate that. I have done everything to make him happy. I do everything he asks of me except wipe his god-damn ass. Don't start blaming me for what he does," I snarled.

"I'm not blaming you for anything. No one is, but maybe you brought up something we need to discuss."

"What?" I huffed.

"You said that you have done everything to make him happy, but what have you done to make yourself happy?"

I need some time to think about that one.

Chapter 26

IT WAS WEEK SEVEN of Andrew's sessions. I waited in my usual place with a glass of white wine in my hand and the bottle close by for an easy refill. I braced for whatever this week's revelation would be.

"Hi. How are the kids?" He sat down close to me, closer than made me comfortable.

I moved a cushion away. "They're fine. Tell me about your meeting?"

"Let's not do this again. I'm making progress."

"Well, no, you're not because you are trying to get out of talking again."

"Fine. I will tell you everything."

"We talked more about Paige. Jul, are you sure you want to hear this?"

"Yup," I said as I poured myself another healthy glass of wine.

"If you insist. Paige was the first person I ever let in. She knew things about me that I never told anyone, not even you."

"Like what?"

"How my father was always telling me I would never measure up. How I was such a disappointment. Jul, I did everything for him, for my mom, and my brothers, and he didn't give a crap about me. No matter how hard I worked, my father only paid attention to my brothers. The only way I could get him to notice me at all was to be perfect, never talk back, and never, ever reveal an emotion that could make me look weak."

"Well, you most certainly are not perfect, and I guess he trained you well because you never show any emotion at all. He must be so fucking proud."

"No, I'm not perfect, and that's my point. Online, no one cares. They don't need me to reassure them that I love them or desire them. I can just be anonymous. You are the only one who knows me, the real me."

"Sorry, but I don't know you at all."

"Don't say that. Yes, you do."

"Anyway, is this all Vito's fault?"

"I'm not blaming my dad. I needed somewhere to cope, and that's what porn was for me. The problem is that every time I try to stop, I end up doing it again. We are working on it, babe; I promise, everything will be better soon."

"What ended up happening to Paige?"

"She left a few days after I told her about my relationship with my dad. I suppose no one wants a weak man."

"Boo-Fucking-Hoo." I grabbed the bottle and went upstairs.

Chapter 27

MY SESSIONS WITH LAURA are helping me think like an individual again instead of half of a dysfunctional couple.

"Perhaps the real battle is figuring out what he can do to change his behavior. You said he needs to escape and be in control, right? Those are the issues he needs to work on with his therapist. Let's spend our time unraveling what is going on with you."

"Ugh, okay."

"So, what will it be this week?" She asked, as if looking at a menu of issues still to be tackled.

"I had book club this week. I don't like it, but it gets me out of the house. This bitch in the group got under my skin. I'm sorry for the language, but I am still fuming."

"What happened that has you so upset?"

"Her name is Terry. We travel in the same circle. I probably would have called her a friend before this happened, but not anymore. In the middle of discussing *Carry On Warrior* and child-rearing difficulties, she tells me I'm a terrible mother. That I'm raising Jack to be bullied."

"What do you mean?"

"That was exactly my question. She brings up something that happened after school the other day. Some boys were wrestling rather aggressively. Jack knows our rules—no hitting of any kind. He looked at me silently, asking what to do. I called him over, not wanting him to be put in a difficult situation as other mothers just stood around talking about the latest episode of Oprah. I'm not okay with it. That is not how I want to raise my son, and it's none of her fucking business."

"You are right." she shook her head in agreement.

"She went on about how I was suffocating Jack. She was saying that I needed to back off, or he was going to turn into a pussy. She didn't use that exact word, but that was what she meant. She, in her infinite wisdom, told me I should read some book about letting boys be boys."

"That is an outdated philosophy. It's parents like that who perpetuate the chain of violence."

"Exactly," I said, relieved she agreed. "If Jack wants or needs to work out aggression, I think we can find more constructive outlets."

"Absolutely."

"Thank you, Laura." The tension began to ease out of my stiff back. "You make me feel almost normal." I laughed at the word 'normal' being associated with me. "I told her I thought she was wrong, and our conversation ended up getting a little heated. I'm rarely confrontational, but really, who the hell does she think she is? My son is highly intelligent, funny, well-behaved, well-adjusted, and loving. I'm passionate about the anti-violence stuff. It's obvious she has never been subjected to living in fear of having the crap beaten out of her. She has no idea what it's like to walk on eggshells, waiting for a blanket of fury to drop. What a closed-minded bitch! She is completely clueless. Isn't it our job as parents to redirect hostility into a more productive outlet?"

"Yes, it is. I'm glad you stood up to her. You are an amazing mother; don't let anybody tell you differently. From what I know about your children, you are doing a remarkable job. Violence is never the way. She is wrong. Plain and simple."

"Thanks. I needed to get that out. It's been pissing me off all week." I took a deep breath. "Can we talk a little about something we touched on last week?"

"Sure. What is it?" she wondered.

"I've been thinking a lot about what I should do to make myself happy. I am ready to do it, but I am having trouble figuring out what 'it' is."

We spent the last fifteen minutes of our session talking about the things I used to enjoy doing and which of them I might be able to bring back into my life.

I left thinking therapy wasn't so bad.

Chapter 28

THE FOLLOWING DAY, I sat on the couch with a child cuddled under each arm, watching *Sesame Street*. How I wished it could stay like that forever—just the three of us. The magic spell was broken by the ringing telephone. I wiggled my way out of my children's warm, loving arms that wrapped around me like an octopus.

"Hello?"

"Hey Jul, how's it going?"

I brightened up at the sound of his voice. "Kev! How is my long-lost friend? I thought you forgot about me."

"Never!"

Kevin had been one of my guy friends off and on for years. I could tell him anything. Once in a while, back in the day, we would kiss too. We were never a couple, only friends, dear friends. He was funny and made me laugh. Sometimes with him. Sometimes at him. He could even make me laugh at myself.

Kevin continually aspires to improve himself. He reads self-help books and goes to seminars, all in the name of mental health. I admire his ability to be introspective and still feel good about who he is.

During our phone call, he told me about his misadventures of rapid dating and his unsuccessful efforts to find his soulmate. I told him about the children's latest successes and repeated any hometown gossip my girls had passed along.

"Mommy, SpongeBob is on. Can we watch it?" yelled Jack from the other room.

"No, sorry, Mister. I'll be right in." I put the phone back to my ear. "Sorry, but I have to go back on duty. Hey, thanks for calling."

"Jul, are you okay?"

"Of course. Aren't I always?"

"I guess. I miss you."

"Miss you too. Bye."

I stood staring at the phone, wondering if I should have confided in him. A moment later, the phone rang again.

"What are you doing Friday night?" Kevin asked.

"Nothing to speak of."

"Come over for a drink."

Much to my surprise, I said, "Yeah, sure. I'd love to."

I had thought I had covered up my misery, but he knew me well enough to hear in my voice that things weren't right.

Many times, over the last few years, I'd doubted myself. I know I have a flair for the dramatic, much like my mom. I'm not always convinced that I see things from their proper perspective. I decided I would tell him, and he could let me know if I was crazy or justified.

Friday came. After tucking my babies into bed, I headed out the door, telling Andrew not to expect me back that night. I intentionally didn't tell him where I was going. If he could mess with my head, I could mess with his.

I pulled up to Kevin's townhouse and sat in my car for a minute to gain my composure. I saw him waving to me out the front door, beckoning me to come in. His familiar smile wiped away any trepidation I had. I went into an all-out sprint and jumped into his arms. Within minutes, we were outside on his deck with a martini in one hand and a joint in the other, relaxing in our familiarity.

"Jul, something is going on. I could hear it in your voice the other day, and now that I see you...you look tired, really tired."

"Thanks. I guess I've lost my little girl charm."

"Not at all. You just look like you have the weight of the world on your shoulders."

Before I could stop myself, I told him the whole story. The unedited version came gushing out. It may have been the alcohol or the pot. Perhaps both. When I finished, I studied his face for a reaction.

"Are you kidding me?" his face was filled with confusion.

"Sorry. Too much information?"

"It's not that. The guy's a jerk."

"Why do you say that?"

"I can't believe he told you he was in love with someone else. What a jackass!"

"That's so funny. That is exactly what I called him the other week."

Kevin knew me well enough to know what that information would do to me, what it would do to anyone, for that matter. I walked over and sat on his lap to be comforted as I cried. Damn, I'd cried far too much over the last decade.

I lifted my head from his shoulder and looked into his sweet blue eyes. Leaning in, I attempted to initiate a kiss. Instead of responding, as he always had in the past, he gently took me by my shoulders and moved me away. I looked at him with tear-stained cheeks and pathetic, bloodshot eyes.

"I'm so sorry." I was embarrassed by what I had just done. He stroked the side of my hair. "Don't be sorry, but I can't be with you. You're still married."

"You're right. That was stupid. I'm stupid. What the fuck is wrong with me?"

"Nothing's wrong with you, but you know as well as I do that if anything happened between us, you would beat yourself up forever. It's not going to fix anything."

"I don't care. I want you to kiss me." Looking at him, I knew he wouldn't give in to temptation. "I'm so lost. What the hell has happened to my life?" Again, I started to cry, and he let me.

We spent the rest of the evening lying on his couch and holding each other.

"Come on," Kevin scolded me. "Stop letting that douche bag get the best of you."

"It's already a done deal. He got it and stomped on it."

"You are stronger than this. Take your life back. If you don't want it with him, find it somewhere else. You can't just roll over. That's not your style."

"Who wants a forty-something-year-old divorced woman with two children? My boobs sag from nursing, I have an enormous scar across my abdomen, and I pee when I laugh." I was enjoying the haze of a solid buzz. Giggling, I squeezed my legs together.

"You'd be surprised. You are bright, beautiful, sexy as hell, funny, and a little nuts, but that's okay. Plenty of men would jump at the opportunity to be with you, as long as you don't pee on their sofa. Trust me." Was he speaking for himself? I wasn't sure. "Before you do anything, you need to decide what you want. Julie, do you even want to save your marriage?"

"Look at you being all serious. Kev, you should have been a therapist. If you were, I would keep you on retainer." I kissed him on the cheek and cuddled up even closer.

I fell asleep wondering why I never fell in love with him. Maybe I should have tried harder with him, and I could have avoided this mess. We slept side by side, holding hands throughout the night.

The following morning, I left with the resolve to make my life better. No one else was going to do that for me. I would gather the strength and courage Kevin had given me and approach my problems head-on. Since miracles don't happen—at least not to me—I would make one of my own.

I walked in the door feeling strong, funny, and still a little sexy for the first time in what seemed like forever. Also, very hungover.

"Hey, glad you're back. Did you have fun?" Andrew asked me with a hug.

"Yeah, I had a very nice time. I think it helped."

I picked up Tess, smothering her with kisses, and hugged Jack so hard, he begged to be let go. Being away from them for even less than twenty-four hours was difficult. We spent the rest of the day playing with Legos and Little People, lost in the innocence of childhood.

After putting the kids to bed, I opened up the conversation. "Let's try to move past this. I really don't want to do this anymore," I said, while pulling the cork from a fresh bottle of Merlot.

"Thank God! Me too." Andrew sighed with relief.

"I need you to be a husband in every sense of the word. Do you think you can do that?"

"What are you talking about? I love you. We are married. What else do you want?"

"I want to laugh again. I want you to date me." I filled my glass to the top.

"Honestly, I have no idea what you're saying. I don't understand what you expect of me."

"I'm saying if you don't want me, I'm sure someone else will." I put my glass down harder than expected; wine jumped out of the glass all over the end table. As I wiped it up, I told him in no uncertain terms, "You'd better hurry up and make up your mind, or it might be too late."

"Too late for what?"

"Too late for us. I may find someone else who is willing to give it all to me."

"I love you. Why do you have to read so much into everything? God, can't we just let it go?" He blustered, his voice filled with aggravation. I downed my glass and poured myself another.

"I want you to say you want me. I want to have sex more than four times a year. I want you to throw me against a wall and make love to me. I want you to go down on me in the kitchen. I want you to fuck me on the floor. I want passion."

"I can't. I'm not that kind of guy."

"So, should I find someone else who is? Should I have an affair?"

"If that's what you have to do."

I was speechless. I went to my room and laid in bed, thinking about what he said. Hadn't I declared a few hours ago that I was going to make my own happiness? Perhaps I was angry, disappointed, and probably not wholly rational or sober, but I decided to do it. What the hell? I needed to figure out with whom I would have my affair. It had to be someone I trusted. It had to be someone who cared about me and someone I cared about as well. I didn't want a fuck and run. I was too old for that.

Kevin was the obvious choice, but he would never agree. He had too much integrity. He loved me too much. The name came to me as if in a news flash. Brandon. It couldn't be anyone else but him. I knew we never stopped caring about each other, and our bond would never be broken regardless of how much time passed. The question was, could I find him, and would he go for what I was going to propose? I downed one last glass of wine and fell asleep.

Chapter 29

"HI JULIE, COME ON in." Laura motioned for me to take my usual seat. "How did everything go?"

"You're not going to believe this," I said, shaking my head in disbelief. "He told me to have an affair. Can you frigging believe it?"

"Really? What are you going to do?"

"Exactly what he said. I'm going to have an affair."

"I think we should talk about this first." Her tone was more doctor-ish than usual.

"Laura, he doesn't want to have sex with me. He doesn't want a physical relationship, and I need one. He is stuck somewhere that I can't go. I don't know what else to do."

"Do you think he meant it?"

"I don't think that is something you say off the cuff. It lets him off the hook, and, at this point, that's fine with me. I'm tired of begging and fighting. You never know; it might work."

"Do you think that's possible?"

"I don't know; it works in movies. Can we drop this for today? I have to tell you what I did last week."

I told her about my night with Kevin.

"He sounds like a great guy. Why didn't you pursue a long-term relationship with him?"

I raised my eyebrows in question.

"Going back a little farther, by your own admission, Brian loved you too and treated you very well, yet you broke up with him."

"I'm not sure. I loved them but not 'L-O-V-E-D' them. I wish I did. Everything would have been so much easier." I took a little time to think about it some more. "They are both so normal. They come from lovely families, have had normal childhoods, as far as I know, and were very cute, but I didn't see a future with them. That intangible 'je ne sais quoi' was missing. Maybe they weren't broken enough. Maybe, because they loved me, I couldn't love them back." I shrugged my shoulders, unable to give any further explanation.

"Self-sabotage?"

"Maybe. Can we return to the possibility of, well, other possibilities?" I was excited at the thought of what may be to come.

"So, will it be Kevin?" she sounded clinical.

"No. He would never do it, but I have an idea who might."

Brandon was an old boyfriend. We met when he was a senior in college at a popular local bar. I was walking out, and he was coming in. I remember it vividly. The place was packed with wall-to-wall people; everyone was pushing and shoving, trying to make their way to order a drink. We brushed up against each other in passing. "Excuse me," I heard him say. I was taken aback by his beautiful smile, perfect white teeth, and the kind of eyes that hypnotize. He was tall with shaggy blonde hair and a commanding presence. "Why are you leaving?" His eyes were pleading for me to stay.

Talk about 'je ne sais quoi!'

I was so blown away by his physicality that I could barely stammer out the words, "My friends are waiting." Danni had me by the arm, dragging me past the exit door. "I have to go. Bye."

As I walked away, I heard him call out, "Hope I run into you again."

Dear God, I hoped so too.

I kicked myself for the rest of the night, thinking I had blown my only chance with the Adonis I had just met. I woke to the phone on my bedstand ringing.

The sun beamed through the crack of the curtains, urging me from my slumber. Groggily, I picked up the receiver.

"Do you have any idea what I went through to find your number?"

"Who is this?" I was trying to clear the alcohol remnants from my system.

"Brandon. We met at Malone's last night. The tall blonde guy who wants to see you again. Ring a bell?"

"How did you get my number?" I wondered out loud while still rubbing the sleep out of my eyes.

"I have my ways," he released a mock sinister laugh. "Now that I have you, what are you doing tonight?"

"I think something with you." I'm sure he could tell I was smiling.

That night was the beginning of our whirlwind romance. We fed on each other's bodies and drank each other's souls. He was the first person with whom I shared my secrets. It came out one night while sitting on his bed.

"I have to tell you something."

"What is it?" he looked at me so tenderly my heart melted.

"I have never told anyone. This is really hard." My voice quivered. I had no idea how he would react. I thought I might lose, scare, or disgust him, but I decided to take the chance and trust him.

I told him everything that had happened to me as a little girl, my father, the men, and how I lost my virginity.

"I wanted you to know. I want you to understand why I get weepy and weird sometimes when we have sex. It's bizarre; I can go months or years without thinking about it, and suddenly, there it is, bright as the sun, and I can't get rid of it. I end up feeling dirty and scared again. It's as if I'm transported right back there. I wish it would go away and stay away." Before I could go on, he kissed away the tears that started to roll down my face.

"I know exactly what you mean. I really do," he whispered.

I understood what he was implying, and my heart broke for him, but I also took comfort knowing we were kindred spirits. We held and kissed each other as if we would die if our physical beings were separated.

"I will never let anyone hurt you ever again. I promise. I will kill them first," he swore.

That was the first night I had ever made love to anyone. With Brandon, I finally understood the difference between sex and making love. Making love wasn't about power or aggression. It was beautiful and all-encompassing. We shared our pains. Our hopes and dreams would bind us together forever.

As with many things that start with speed and passion, we ended almost as quickly. We all have our demons to battle, and Brandon fought his with drugs. When we met, he was sober, but unfortunately, he didn't stay that way. His old friend, shame, enticed him into the darkness. The drugs stole him away so quickly that I didn't realize what was happening. It wasn't long before he was completely lost to me.

During our time together, we had something that many could only dream of. It was a trust, a connection, which couldn't be put into words. To this day, he holds a precious piece of my heart.

For many years, we stayed in touch. Perhaps it was more than that. We had the kind of friendship that lends itself to certain physical benefits. Neither of us was ever able to let go completely. We were 'friends' until I met Andrew. My love for Andrew was so strong that I severed all communications with Brandon. After Andrew's affair proposal, I was set to correct that.

"Tread very carefully. You can't undo what you are contemplating." Laura's voice was full of warning.

"Thanks, Doc. I'll try to behave," I said, the words oozing with sarcasm.

I Googled Brandon and found his contact details remarkably easy. He was working as an insurance agent in New City, New York. I dashed off a quick email and hit send before I talked myself out of it.

Julie: Just came across your website, so I thought I'd say hi. How is everything going? I'm sorry we lost touch. - Julie

Within seconds, a response came back.

Brandon: I can't believe it's you! How did you find me? Last I heard, you got married.

My heart raced reading his words.

Julie: I have my ways. If I recall correctly, I remember you found me years ago.

Brandon: Ha! You are absolutely right. That was one of the best things I ever did. Tell me, how are you?

Julie: I'm good. I'm married with 2 kids. I drive a mom-mobile and living a bizarrely adequate life?

Brandon: Adequate? That's not exactly a ringing endorsement of a happily married woman.

Julie: Did I say anything about being happy?

The blatant flirtation made me feel young and giddy.

Brandon: Touché

Julie: Now you. Are you happily married with little towheads running around?

Brandon: No children. Too scared to procreate. Could you imagine a little me running around? God help us all. I did get married. She's a lovely woman, but to be honest, she was a replacement for you.

Right after I heard about you getting married, I proposed. I thought I had lost you forever.

Julie: I'm not sure that is even possible. You will always be part of my soul. This may sound weird, but do you want to get together one night for drinks and catch up?

Brandon: I feel like I'm having some weird drug-induced dream.

Julie: Are you still doing drugs? My heart sank in disappointment.

Brandon: No, no, really, I'm not. It was just a comparison. I would love to see you.

Julie: How about the bar at the Sheraton on 17? 8:00? Wednesday?

Brandon: I can't wait.

Neither could I. I told Andrew I was going out to visit my mother that night. Of course, I took her advice and wore clean and very sexy black lace panties, just in case.

I was nervous but also excited. Brandon and I had always had a comfortable relationship, but that was long ago.

When I arrived, I peeked through the window, trying to spot him before I rounded the corner to make my entrance. I could see him sitting at the bar drinking a beer and watching the football game. His hairline had receded slightly, and his six-pack looked more like a spare tire, but he was still my Brandon. The way he stroked the moisture off his glass made me think of his fingers touching my body.

The longer I stood there, the more nervous I became. Catching my reflection in the lobby mirror,

I did a quick once over to make sure my silk blouse hung just right and walked in.

He looked up as I entered, and a huge smile crossed his face. God, I missed that smile.

"Hi!" his voice had an edge of tension buried within. "You haven't changed a bit."

"Hi, yourself." I gave him a quick peck on the cheek.

"Can I order you a drink?"

"Sure."

"Stoli and grapefruit, right?"

"Impressive memory, but I think I'll stick with wine tonight."

He had put on about twenty pounds and wore glasses, but he had the same beautiful and loving blue eyes where I had once gotten lost. Immediately, I could see a fire still burned in us both. We talked and laughed for hours, reminiscing about old times. It was as if we had stepped into the past and were kids again. The more we drank, the more I allowed my guard to come down.

"Letting you go was the biggest mistake of my life," he confessed.

"Things happen. Don't beat yourself up. Is everything going okay with you?"

"I thought it was until you emailed."

We went from a cordial distance to our arms and legs being entwined. We breathed the same air. But Kevin's voice kept popping into my head, and I got scared that I might regret what I knew was about to happen. Abruptly, I stood, unlocking myself from our coupling. "I'm sorry, but I have to go. Please let me pick up the tab."

We walked to my car in silence. The reminder of my real life was sitting with two booster seats in the back, a floor full of Cheerios, and sippy cups half-filled with sour milk. I reached up to hug him. He met me halfway and kissed me softly on the lips. The nerves in my body began to tingle. My brain told me I should pull away, but instead, I melted into him. We stayed in that euphoric state for at least ten minutes until he broke our embrace. I stood dazed in the aftermath. He took my hand and led me back inside the hotel, giving me a sideways glance and a devilish smile. He walked over to the front desk and asked for a room. I watched the scene play out as if it were happening to someone else.

Brandon returned to my side and led us inside an ordinary room. In front of me stood a king-sized bed, a double dresser, a wall-mounted television, and a desk. My head was cloudy from the alcohol and the charged sexual atmosphere. I heard the door close behind me, but before I was able to turn around, his arms were holding me by the waist, and he was kissing my neck. Oh, God, he remembered how I love having my neck kissed. The blood in my veins was surging like molten lava. It was all I could do not to lose myself completely. I caught our reflection in the mirror and couldn't believe what I was witnessing or its effect on me. The erotic sight of my lover holding me stirred up my passion quickly. I turned and kissed him on the lips, pressing my body against his. His hands were all over me. He was caressing every curve. It was as if he was seeing if everything was where he had left it. And it was. I was his to reclaim.

He picked me up and placed me on the bed. Slowly, he pulled off my black shirt and kissed my bare shoulders as the silk dropped away. Next was my lace bra, after which he ran his mouth softly over my breasts and grazed my nipples with his teeth. He unbuttoned my jeans and removed them with such expertise I barely had time to notice. When he got to my lace panties, he slid them over my hips and down my legs and kissed me there as well. He was so amazing at it that even if I wanted him to stop; I don't think my body would have allowed him. My body ached with pleasure, lost in a tidal wave of ecstasy. I hadn't had a fulfilling orgasm in eons. The moans I let out were so audible; they surprised me.

If this was what I could expect from having an affair, I was all in. I wanted to return the favor, but he wouldn't let me. He said the night was going to be about me, and it was all night long.

Sometime around eleven o'clock, I made a quick call home, saying I would stay the night with my mother and be home early in the morning. I hung up and crawled back into bed with Brandon.

I spent the night in his arms and his mouth. It was one of the most sensual nights of my life. In the morning, I was exhausted, satiated, and smiling. Much to my surprise, I didn't feel guilty at all. Why should I? I was being an obedient wife and doing as I was told.

I returned home, and Andrew did not ask a single question. I couldn't believe how easy it had been. I jumped in the shower to start my day, as I always did. I took the children to school, did the laundry, and cooked dinner as if nothing had ever happened.

But something had happened, and I had a smile on my face all day as evidence.

Two days later, I received an email from Brandon.

Brandon: The other night was amazing. I had forgotten how well we fit together. I'm sorry I haven't been in touch sooner, but I needed to figure out what to do. I can't believe I can still feel this way, and I wonder how different our lives might have been. I miss you. When can I see you?

I replied without hesitation.

Julie: It was wonderful to see you, and I loved being held in your arms again. Thank you for an amazing night. Before this goes any further, I think we need to talk about what we want from this, so no one gets hurt. I can't wait to see you again. J

Brandon and I were destined only to be lovers. Although he denied it, he was still involved with drugs, making it impossible for us to have anything more than a physical relationship. I would never allow him fully into my life. I wouldn't do that to my children.

Brandon: Are you free to meet me this Friday?

Julie: In fact, I am. I'll bring dinner. What's your favorite thing to eat?

Brandon: You! See you Friday. L, B

Back to Laura, I went.

"Hi," I said with a smile that let her know that I had something decadent to discuss.

"Hi Julie, come on in. You seem happy today." She looked at me suspiciously.

"I am. I contacted Brandon, and we met."

"And how do you feel about that?"

"Incredible. I feel sexy. Desired. It has been so long since someone went down on me, and it was AMAZING!"

"Yes, done properly; it is amazing." She said clinically, but with the smile of a woman who is familiar with this kind of pleasure.

"Laura, honestly, if you had asked me five years ago if I would ever have had an affair, my answer would have been an unequivocal, 'No,' but look at me now. I'm doing it, and I have no desire to stop." I threw myself back in the chair. "God, what I have been missing?"

It goes to show that nobody ever knows what's going to happen. That was the day I embarked on an eighteen-month hot and steamy affair that would leave me with as many questions as when I started, perhaps more.

Remarkably, during that time, Andrew and I were getting along better than we had in years. Perhaps because I was getting 'some' regularly, but more likely because I was no longer sitting around helpless. I was controlling something. Once again, I had that familiar sense of power.

Brandon and I met once a month under the guise of a book club. I would read a book and go to a 'book club' for group discussion. We had no conversations about literary choices, authors, or storylines. When we did speak, it was about how much we once loved each other and how, when we are together, nothing else mattered.

Our ritual continued. He would register for the room, text me the number; I would knock twice; he would open the door, drag me inside, and ravage me. We would have sex three times in three hours, and he would cum each time. I'm not sure how many women can relate to that sort of achievement, but for me, it was like getting an A-plus on a final exam.

We were both behaving boldly and cocky, so comfortable with our arrangement. We took it a step further and went away for a weekend. Our respective spouses thought we were going to Atlantic City with friends.

We met in the Borgata Hotel and Casino's lobby and checked in, pretending we were married. The bellhop showed us to our room, and when he opened the door, Brandon carried me over the threshold. Something Andrew had never done.

"We never did this for real, but I've always wanted to," he smiled and kissed me deliciously on the lips.

We spent eighteen hours in bed, making love, watching television, and sleeping. It was a vacation from life.

We were two old friends, finding comfort from the world together. It didn't feel wrong. In fact, it felt natural. We cared about each other. I would go so far as to say we loved each other. Love in a friendly and non-threatening way. It worked for the two of us. Actually, all four of us, and Laura didn't think it was a crazy solution. My theory was if my therapist didn't think it was wrong and my husband didn't mind, then why should I be the one to feel guilty?

The first year was incredible. Both our marriages were flourishing. I didn't harp at him about his drug use, and he didn't make me feel bad about myself.

If I could merge Brandon's unyielding sensuality and Andrew's responsibility, I would have the perfect man. I was so close to having it all.

Chapter 30

BRANDON AND I HAD been together for an entire year without anyone getting suspicious. After a night of vivid dreams, I awoke aroused and sent him a text to make sure he knew what was on my mind.

Julie: I'm so happy to have you in my life again. I want you in my mouth and smell the musky scent between your legs. I ache for your touch along the curves of my body. If you were here right now, there would be no denying how turned on I am. Can we try for later? Call me.

An hour passed without a response. I continued with my day, cursing him under my breath.

Three hours passed and still nothing. So, I called him.

"Hey, what's going on? Are you mad at me?"

"Karen, read your text." He said with an edge in his voice.

"What?" I went into a full panic.

"I was in the kitchen, pouring my coffee, when she came in and threw my phone at my head."

"Oh my God!" I began to tremble.

"She called me a fucking cheating bastard and ran out of the house."

"Isn't your phone password protected? Andrew's is."

"No, it's not, and she read it."

"Does she know who I am? Is she going to come after me?" I asked, giving no thought to how this would affect him.

"I don't think so." He didn't sound convincing and didn't seem upset that his life just blew up, but I was.

"What do we do now?"

"We're going to have to lie low for a while. I'll let you know when things die down. I'm going to miss you. Bye."

Damn! What if she showed up here? What if the children were home when she did? What if the neighbors found out?

I was pissed at both Brandon and myself. I was pissed at Andrew, too. It was easy for me to blame everyone else, but the truth was it was my fault we got caught. I got sloppy and comfortable. I got stupid, as usual.

Every day I waited for Karen to show up at my door, but, thankfully, she never did. After about three months, I emailed Brandon again. Perhaps I was self-destructive, or I missed the excitement our affair brought into my life, but I didn't want to give it up. Not yet.

Julie: Hi! Is everything OK?

Brandon: Yes. Are you OK?

Julie: I'm fine. That was close. I can't wait to hear how you talked your way out of it.

Brandon: It wasn't easy, but I bullshit well. I'll tell you all about it when I see you. Free Monday night?

Julie: Yes! What is wrong with us? You'd think we would have learned our lesson. Oh, well.

Brandon: We're two idiots. Glad you're still on board.

Julie: Yup, still on board, and yes, we are two idiots, but love you anyway.

Things never returned to how they had been; reality had snuck in and sucked the fun out of our affair. We tried to ignore what we both knew to be true. Our affair was over.

The calls stopped, as did the emails and texts; that was the end.

My relationship with Brandon was about sex, excitement, comfort, and revenge. I had fallen back into the trap of sex for attention. Sex for power. Sex for love. I came to realize that I wanted more than sex. I wanted to experience everything with one person. All I had accomplished was finding a new place to hide temporarily from my life.

I needed to find a way to keep myself occupied that didn't involve men or sex. I needed to find something that fulfilled me. The time had come to be more than Andrew's wife, Jack and Tess's mother, or Brandon's lover. I needed to be Julie, but I didn't know who that was.

From the time I was a small girl and my grandparents had taken me to the Met and the Guggenheim, I had loved the world of art. It was there I was introduced to Monet, Cezanne, Renoir, Calder, and Warhol. I dabbled in creating a bit in high school and college, but fell to the wayside. Being among art has always been soothing and creating art, liberating. Maybe it would lead me to my true self again, whoever she was.

I enrolled in an art class at a small studio in town. We began by imitating some famous masters. I loved the slipperiness of the wet clay gliding through my fingers while studying Rodin and the dust chalk left behind when we worked on Degas. I would pass a brush over a clean white canvas, leaving a trace of myself behind. I was entranced by the depth of color and the texture of form of the different mediums. I was starting to find my happiness.

Chapter 31

ANDREW WAS WORKING HARD to become the man I had always wanted him to be. He was growing, learning to listen, and more involved in the children's lives. He had returned to the family nest to take his place by my side, but I was no longer there.

I would visit New York City one weekend a month and see the most recent exhibits. It was the only real me time I had. I left in the morning, returning shortly before dinner.

"So, how was the museum? Anything interesting today?" he sounded genuinely curious.

"Yeah, they had an intriguing exhibit featuring South American artists from the late 1800s. It was something. You don't see much of that in the mainstream museums around here."

"That sounds interesting. Remember when we used to go together, before kids?"

"Yeah, we used to have fun, didn't we? That was a long time ago when we had stuff to talk about, or if we didn't, at least we enjoyed each other's company."

"Well, I still enjoy your company. I'll ask my mom if she can babysit one Saturday, and we can go in together. Would that be okay?"

"We can talk about it. I'm tired. I think I need to go to sleep now." Andrew got up to go, but before he did, I touched his arm, "Thanks for taking an interest."

He left with a genuine smile. I could tell because the right side of his mouth curled slightly more than his left when it was real.

Chapter 32

THE FOLLOWING DAY, I was sitting on the cracked brown couch reading another outdated copy of People magazine. I heard her familiar voice say, "Hi, Julie. Come on in."

Sometimes I look forward to our weekly sessions, but other times I just want to call it quits. This week, I'm okay with it.

"So, how's it going?" It was her usual question once we'd settled into our spots in her office.

"Not bad," I smiled. "I've had a decent week. The kids are great, as always. Jack is such a love. He has so many wonderful attributes, but I worry about him. He expects so much of himself, too much. Unfortunately, he is a lot like me, which scares the shit out of me. I have to find a way to help him relax so it doesn't become a burden. Sarah says he is so sweet he makes her teeth ache. God bless that little boy.

"Tess has me wrapped around her little finger. She can make me so furious one moment and makes me love her like no other the next. She's going to be all right. She has a balance of heart and bravado. She is not going to be your average girl! I tell Andrew all the time, don't break her. She needs to be tough and resilient. No one will fuck with her that way. It's hard for him, though. They get along like water and oil. Andrew is being sweet and taking things a little more in stride. To top it off, I think I got a little sleep. So yeah, it was a decent week. I might even be, dare I say it... happy." However, I neglected to tell her my sleep came with a tumbler of vodka and a pill, but she didn't need to know everything.

"Sounds like progress. Tell me what's happening with Andrew."

"Well, I'm starting to like him again, but only as my friend. I don't want to rip his head off anymore. I think it's progress, but I'm still not in love with him, and I doubt I ever will be again."

"What makes you say that?"

"I can't trust him, so I can't love him. Even after everything we have been through, it bothers me that I'm hurting him. It's admirable he is working so hard to change for me, but it's too late."

"It's never too late. If you don't want to make it work, that's one thing, but if you want to, you can still save your marriage."

"That's just it—I'm not sure I still want to be in my marriage," I said, cringing at my own words.

Chapter 33

AT MY NEXT VISIT with Laura, we spoke of how I wished I could love Andrew and how I miss the fantastic sex with Brandon. We discussed why the world and the people in it still often piss me off. Overall, we had a decent session until she wanted to revisit the events that occurred at the little house on North Cottage Drive. I don't like going there and avoid it at all costs. Blessedly, our time ran out before I had to make the trip.

The following Saturday was a beautiful day, and I set off on one of my monthly visits to New York. There was an exclusive showing of privately owned paintings that had never been exhibited for public viewing. I was bursting with excitement as the New Jersey Transit train pulled into Penn Station. I quickly hurried through the maze of tunnels, past the Krispy Kreme donut stand, the blind old man playing the tambourine, and set off past the thousands of pedestrians in my quest for my liberation.

I meandered my way down Madison Avenue and entered the tiny gallery sandwiched between two retail stores. It was not much larger than the downstairs of my house. Looking around, I saw wall upon wall of paintings that sprang to life. I was drifting in a sea of Monet. Taking my time, I viewed each from different distances and angles—altering my vantage point could change my perception of the subject matter.

I sat on a wooden bench, wondering about Monet as a man. Did painting take him to a place far from the extreme emotions that often haunt great artists? Was the use of color an escape from the darkness that surrounded him? I was alone in my extreme emotional intensity for much of my life, but not when I was with the artists.

On the walls hung dozens of paintings done of Giverny. Looking at each one, I never grew tired of the gardens made with the varying use of color and light. My favorite was *Camille Monet In the Garden at the House in Argenteuil.* Camille, Monet's first wife, is walking down the path away from the golden, sunlit house in the background into a shadowy foreground. The contrast to the darker, more subdued colors made the house behind her take on an almost pink hue. I wondered why Camille was leaving and where she was going. Why was she cast in shadow? Was it representative of her living in Monet's shadow?

It dawned on me that I didn't need to know why anyone painted what they did. All that mattered was how it made me feel. It's possible I didn't have to understand why I felt what I did all the time; I only needed to know how to control it.

As I stood, I could sense someone was staring at me. At first, I tried to ignore the sensation, but the unrelenting gaze made me self-conscious as it continued to burn a hole in my back. Breaking my study, I turned to acknowledge the owner of those eyes. When I did, they were oddly familiar. They belonged to a man I had known when I was dating Brandon. I racked my brain, trying to recover his name. Damn, was it Paul, Mike, John, Peter? Yes! It came back to me. His name was Mark. Mark Sullivan. I was relieved to have it surface, but with it came the memory that he was an asshole.

"Julie?" He said, sounding surprised as if he hadn't been standing behind me for the last ten minutes, willing me to turn around.

"Mark? Funny running into you here." I mimicked his surprised tone. We exchanged pleasantries for a moment while I drifted off, remembering the last time I had seen him.

It was the last day of Brandon's senior year in college, and I was still crazy in love. We had planned a romantic evening for our last night before he had to return home. During the day, Mark convinced Brandon to go on a road trip but promised to have him back by seven o'clock to have our date. That evening seven o'clock came, as did eight, nine, and ten, and Brandon was nowhere in sight. I sat in front of his dorm, waiting for him. At ten-thirty that night, he came running up the walkway, tripping over his apologies. It seemed that old reliable Mark had taken off on Brandon and left him two hours away.

"I'm so sorry, Honey. That shithead left me stranded. He took off with some chick. I took a bus and ran the last mile. Please, don't be mad."

As he finished the story and we got up to leave, Mark pulled up in his blue '68 Camaro convertible. "Yo, Big B, jump in. Let me buy you a beer. No harm, no foul?"

"Don't think so," Brandon said much more calmly than I would have.

"Dude, I'm sorry, but I got an offer I couldn't refuse. She was insanely hot. Did you check out her rack? Wowzah! You understand how it is." He laughed and gestured my way and said, "Oh no, are you in the doghouse?"

"Mark, get the hell out of here." Brandon was not buying his lame attempt at an apology.

I rolled my eyes at Brandon. "God, what a complete douche bag!"

Once my trip down memory lane ended, I realized Mark was waiting for a reply to a question I hadn't heard.

"I'm sorry. Sometimes I get lost in the work."

"I can be the same way. I love art. In fact, I recently bought a Warhol."

"Really? Bully for you." I blurted out flippantly. He was so pretentious.

We continued to walk through the exhibit. We weren't actually walking together as much as he was following me. As we made our way to the exit, I held out my hand to shake his. "Do you have time to join me for a drink?"

I wanted to say no but yes because I couldn't stand the thought of seeing Andrew's pathetic face.

We sat outside at a cafe around the corner from the museum. He ordered a Kettle One and soda and a glass of Chardonnay for me. We sipped our drinks, enjoying the lovely day as the parade of people strolled by. I learned a lot about him in that short time.

"So, where are you living these days?" I asked, trying to fill up the quiet.

"I'm in Chicago. I live with my nine-year-old son."

"You have a child?" I was surprised. The man I had once known was too selfish to care about anyone but himself.

"Yeah, here's his picture." He took out a wallet-sized baseball photo and then a football one. The pride he took in his son was evident in his eyes.

"You and your wife must be very proud."

"Oh, I'm not married. We divorced a few years ago." I wasn't surprised but politely replied, "I'm sorry to hear that."

"Before I say anything else, I have to apologize. I was an asshole in college. I'm very sorry about causing problems between you and Brandon. I was young and immature."

"Thanks, I appreciate that."

I found myself smiling at him. The man I was looking at was not the jerk I had known back in the day. He was a well-dressed, handsome, divorced father who loved his child.

He told me a little about his business. It had something to do with the financial sector, but I wasn't fully paying attention. From what I was able to make out, he'd become a guru in corporate leveraged buyouts, whatever that is. When my glass was empty, I excused myself.

"Thank you for the drink, but I have to be going now."

"It was really nice to catch up. Can I have your number, and maybe next time I'm in town, we can get together?" His eyes had a little sparkle in them, and his forehead crinkled in a way that made him look innocent. In another life, I would have stayed, but instead, I wrote my number on his napkin, thinking it would amount to nothing.

"Thanks for the drink. Take care of your boy."

"I will," he said. Before I turned the corner, I glanced over my shoulder, and he was still watching me.

The rest of the day, I had a bounce in my step. I walked in the door to see Andrew's sullen face, a sink filled with dirty dishes, and my children screaming they were hungry.

Chapter 34

THE START OF THE holiday season was upon us. The world was busy making plans, and so was I. Thanksgiving, Christmas, and New Year's would be upon us soon. Andrew and I were having twenty people for Thanksgiving as usual. It was a traditional Italian feast. We'd start the meal with antipasto, next pumpkin ravioli in butter and sage sauce, followed by the main course of turkey with sausage and apple stuffing, mashed potatoes, sauteed zucchini, candied carrots, and of course, sweet potato casserole topped with miniature marshmallows. It was a lot of hard work, but we had the meal down to a science.

Preparations were well underway at least a week in advance. The turkey was ordered from a free-range farm, the wine was picked up from the local liquor store, and much of the food items were purchased. We bought and prepped the vegetables the day before and made the sweet potato casserole. Our table was set for twenty with our wedding china, crystal, and silver.

We welcomed Andrew's family together at the door with a smile and a kiss. We laughed at the stories being told by our guests and even told a few of our own. Glasses were filled while plates were emptied. We called each other "honey," smiled, and laughed. No one had an inkling that our marriage was in trouble.

Christmas came, and again, we went through the motions. We cut down a tree from the local farm and sang Christmas carols as we decorated. I was still trying to lose myself in the normalcy of it all.

Five o'clock on Christmas morning, I could hear the children chanting to open their presents as a few of my favorite morning scents permeated the air.

I came downstairs to find the three of them ginning at me and a buffet of croissants, boiled eggs, maple bacon, and fresh fruit on the table.

We took turns opening gifts, which was our tradition. When we got to the last one, Andrew picked it up and handed it to me. It was a small gold bag with the name of our local jewelers imprinted on it.

Giving him a sideways glance of disapproval, I slowly opened the bag and the long velvet box within. The lid creaked as I raised it. Glimmering inside was a beautiful diamond tennis bracelet.

"Andrew, you shouldn't have."

"I saw it and couldn't resist. May I put it on you?"

The children's eyes sparkled almost as much as the diamonds. I stammered "sure," uncomfortably, since the little eyes were upon me.

"Yay." Screamed the children in unison.

The rest of the day continued as it always had in the past. I had not forgotten that our life was a mess, but I did want to enjoy what I could.

At the end of the long day, we put the children to bed when they could no longer keep their eyes open. As I headed to my bedroom, Andrew took my hand. "Can we go downstairs and talk?" I followed him without answering.

"Come sit next to me, Jul," he said, tapping the space next to him. "Today was amazing. Everything felt like it used to."

"Andrew, a string of diamonds is not going to fix us."

"I know that. That's not why I gave them to you, but today was wonderful. I can't throw this all away. I won't."

"Andrew..."

"Just hear me out. Do you think you can give me one more year to show you that we can overcome our problems? I want to prove to you that we are supposed to be together. I want to prove we aren't a mistake."

"I don't know. It's already been a long time, and I'm not getting any younger. I want to start over while I still can."

"Come on! We have come this far. What's one more year? If not for me, then for the kids," he begged.

"That's not fair." After a few minutes, I realized he was right. We had two incredibly small, yet enormous, reasons to try everything to make our marriage work. "One year." We shook hands as if sealing a business deal.

A short time after Christmas, I was meeting my friends in New York for dinner and drinks. Andrew had also made plans to meet his friends. We went our separate ways but planned to go home together.

The babysitter showed up, and I ran to catch the 4:45 train to Manhattan. The girls and I met at a trendy bar in the village, hugging and kissing as old friends do. Toasts were made to new children, jobs, the past, and the future. We spent hours reminiscing about the good old days and the less than good ones. We were toasting to anything and everything.

"Here's to Mary, who is looking quite contrary." I raised my glass, dripping my drink all over the floor.

"Here's to Danni with the terrific fanny." Mary smashed her glass into mine.

"Here's to Kristy, who makes me misty." Danni added her glass to the mess.

"Here's to Julie. Hey, I can't think of a rhyme for Julie," Kristy whined.

"It's Juliaaanne," I said, dragging it out to give it an air of elegance and then burst out laughing.

There is nothing in the world like being with old friends. They are the ones with whom I shared my high school dramas and college failures. Before we knew it, it was one o'clock in the morning and time to call it an evening. I texted Andrew that I was ready to go, and he responded that he was coming to our bar to pick me up.

"Oh, I wish this didn't have to end." I gave each of the girls a hug.

"Let's try to get together next month. We'll go to a hot new club opening in midtown soon. We'll dress like sluts and pretend we're twenty," Mary said, shaking her voluptuous tatas.

"You're on! I'll miss you guys!" I hated saying goodbye to them. They piled into a cab, and I waved as they drove off. When they were out of sight, I went back inside to wait for my husband to arrive.

An hour passed, and Andrew never materialized. I must have called fifteen times, sent half a dozen texts, and all went unanswered. With every passing moment, my anger increased. My chest tightened, and my throat closed in a fury. My teeth were starting to clench just as I was alerted to a new text message. It's about time, I thought, flipping my phone open, ready to read Andrew's latest lame excuse, but it wasn't Andrew.

Mark: Hi, how's it going?
Julie: Fine. What can I do for you?
Mark: No need to be so formal. I'm just saying hi.
Julie: Hi.
Mark: What are you doing?
Julie: I'm at The Red Lion. Waiting for hubby to show up and go home, but he's late.
Mark: Don't think he's coming.

I found it rather presumptuous of him to remark when he didn't know Andrew and hardly knew me. I didn't return his message. A half-hour later, my phone chimed again. I answered quickly, hoping it was Andrew.

Mark: Did he show yet?

He was so smug, but I was flattered that he was concerned. At least someone was. A half-hour later, another message came.

Mark: Hey Stubborn, look out the window.

Outside sat a black Lincoln town car with a driver waiting.

Mark: Get in and go home.

I climbed into the town car that Mr. Sullivan had arranged. I was still annoyed at Andrew but made myself comfortable and sent a text back.

Julie: Thanks for the ride. I don't know how you did it, but happy you did. You're a decent guy.

Mark: Yeah, but don't tell anyone.

Julie: Your secret is safe with me.

On the way home, we continued to text each other freely. It was fun and innocent.

Andrew eventually made his way home that night. He had been too drunk to answer his phone and didn't even remember speaking with me. His friends led him to the house and threw him in our front door. In the morning, I found him passed out in the foyer with drool running out of the corner of his mouth. I picked him up off the floor and led him to the couch, where he would be able to spend the day nursing the hangover he was sure to be suffering from.

Chapter 35

THE HOLIDAYS WERE OVER, and Jack and Tess were back in school. I returned to my regularly scheduled life and went back to see Laura.

"How are the classes going?"

"Good," I said, not meeting her eyes.

"Julie, it looks like you have something on your mind," she was obviously very good at what she does.

I took a deep breath. I didn't want to tell her, but she was my doctor, and I understood it would only benefit me if I did.

"Something happened the last time I went to New York. I think I may have met someone."

"Really?"

"Andrew got drunk and forgot to meet me. It doesn't bode well for reconciliation. At least, not in my book. This is the same man who begged me to give our marriage another year." I shook my head in disgust.

I found myself daydreaming about Mark and the charge that electrified my body on the way home the other night when it became apparent that he was interested in me. It was a sensation I wanted to have again. I loved how he took charge and made sure I got home safely. Could he have changed? It appeared to be the case.

I picked up the phone to send a text, but didn't know what to say. 'Hi' sounded innocuous enough. My heart was racing. I wondered if he would answer. Did I want him to? Of course, I did.

Within a minute, I had a reply, and my heart skipped a beat.

Mark: Hey there.

I wasn't sure where to take the conversation, so I began asking random unimportant questions just to get the flow going until he put me out of my misery.

Mark: Do you want to get together again?

I looked at my children playing on the swings. I took note of all the surrounding mothers with their Lulu Lemon ensembles and replied to him.

Julie: I'd like that.

We made a plan to meet in New York again several weeks later. While waiting for the day to come, we began what I can only describe as a relationship of sorts.

The messages that began with casual banter took on a more probing tone. He would ask questions looking for personal information, and I answered. We promised each other total honesty. I lived up to my end. I'm unsure if he lived up to his.

A month into our "courtship," he started a conversation that brought us to another level.

Mark: Hi, what are you doing?
Julie: Having a cocktail, you?
I was beginning to relax.
Mark: Having fun with you. Can I ask a personal question?
Julie: Sure
Mark: If you could change one thing in your life, what would it be?
I probably should not have answered it since I was already tipsy.
Julie: I wish my husband had loved me on our wedding day, and my life wasn't a lie.
Mark: Wow. He must be a fool.
Julie: Your turn.
Mark: I wish my marriage didn't fail.
Julie: I'm so sorry. Would you remarry?
Mark: I'd like to. I'd ask you, but you're taken.
Julie: For now.
I was giving away more than I should have.
Mark: Hum, interesting.
I imagined his smile as I read his reply.

We continued our conversation late into the night. He told me all about how he wanted the chance to find someone to share his world. He said he didn't date much. He didn't have the time. He loved staying home and being with the people who mattered most. He said everything I could have wanted to hear. It was almost as if he had known.

Whenever I heard from him, I felt like a teenager being pursued by a cute guy. My heart was involved with Mark before I even realized it. I wanted him to be special. For us to be special. Unsure if we would be friends, lovers, or perhaps neither, I needed to find out.

The day came for us to meet. I found him in front of the Central Park Carousel, as we had planned. We walked hand in hand along the winding paths, eating warm pretzels. He told me how he had always dreamed of meeting someone like me. Someone who spoke with such honesty and passion that awoke a part of him he had thought was gone long ago.

The time had come for me to return home. He asked if he could kiss me as I was about to leave. I said no, but I desperately wanted to say yes.

On my way home, the texts began again.

Mark: I can't let this go. I can't let you go. Please come away with me.

Julie: I can't! This is crazy.

Part of me wanted it to happen so badly, but the other part, the more rational side, understood it could lead to trouble.

Mark: Yes, you can; it will be innocent. I want to get to know you better. I will be at my place in Naples next month. Please come. I'll put you in a hotel if you want, and I'll make all the arrangements. You won't have to lift a finger.

Julie: This isn't a good idea.

Mark: I'm used to getting what I want and can be very persuasive.

Julie: I may not take that much convincing.

Flirting was one thing, but going to his home was something entirely different. He didn't want to take no for an answer, and I didn't want to give it.

That night, I brought it up to Andrew. "Remember that guy Mark I was telling you about, the one I saw at the Monet show?"

"Yeah," he said, barely listening.

"He has a place in Naples. It sounds fabulous, and he asked me to come down next month. You don't mind if I go, do you?" I was ready with a list of reasons why he should let me, but I didn't need them.

"Of course, I don't mind. Am I invited too?"

"No."

"Okay, just thought I'd ask."

I was confused by his compliance and told him more, thinking he surely would raise some concern after hearing more details. "He's going to fly me down, and I'll stay at his house." I waited for him to say something, but he didn't, so I continued.

"Oh, by the way, he was going to send his jet for me, but it's out of service for the next few weeks, so he'll be flying me first class," I said, figuring now he would object.

"Wow! Do you think he might fly me out to the World Series next year on his plane? That would be so cool! I've always wanted to fly on a private jet."

"You're so fucked up, Andrew," I yelled in disgust.

"What's the matter? I was only saying if he's that generous, maybe he would do a favor for you."

"Aren't you jealous at all?" I couldn't wrap my head around his behavior.

"Should I be?"

"Well, I guess not."

I couldn't understand how he claimed to love me and wanted to grow old with me, yet virtually give his stamp of approval on an affair—or should I say, another affair.

Honestly, did he believe that two consenting adults tucked away on a beach would be purely platonic? If he did, he was a bigger fool than I thought. Unsure whether to hit him for saying I could go or hug him for the same reason, I decided to do nothing at all. If he didn't want me, I knew someone who might. Any steps we had made toward building a new future disappeared. Andrew didn't care enough to stop me, so I was going to teach him a lesson and have a little fun.

While sitting still next to Andrew, I sent Mark a message.

Julie: OK, you're on.

I decided not to see Laura for a while—I was going to handle things myself. By her admission, I was doing well, and frankly, I was afraid she might try to talk me out of going with Mark.

He told me of his plans to hire a yacht to take us out in the gulf to see the sunset. We spoke about how we would spend hours relaxing while drinking champagne and eating caviar. I still couldn't believe what was happening and what I was doing.

We had three weeks for the excitement to build. The text messaging became utterly out of control. So much so, Tess started walking around with her toy cell phone, calling and texting her pre-school friends. So caught up in what was happening, I didn't notice I was doing the same thing Andrew had done. I was stepping out of our family for someone I barely knew on the other end of a digital signal.

Our conversations were getting more provocative.

Julie: What are you doing?
Mark: Thinking of you.
Julie: What about me?
Mark: You naked. Maybe?
Julie: No promises.
Mark: I can hope, can't I?
Julie: I suppose.

A few nights later, he asked an interesting question.

Mark: Would you ever consider moving?
Julie: I suppose if it was for the right reason.
Mark: Fair enough.
Julie: Are you thinking about if things work out between us?
Mark: Maybe. Is that okay?
Julie: I can't think about that yet. This whole thing has taken me by surprise.
Mark: I was just thinking out loud. Hope I didn't scare you.
Julie: No. I don't scare that easily.
Mark: Good. Did I tell you I'm building a new house?

Perhaps he was looking for someone to help fill the void in his life, and I excelled at doing that.

One night, after a couple of glasses of wine, I was frisky and wanted to share it with someone.

Julie: Hi, you awake?

He was quick to respond.

Mark: Yup, what are you doing?
Julie: Thinking of Naples.
Mark: I'm excited!

Julie: Me too. BTW, I think you're sexy.
Mark: Really? I think you are too.
Julie: Thanks. Yummy might be better verbiage.

I sucked on my lower lip as I typed, knowing I had passed the point of no return.

Mark: That implies taste.
Julie: Yes, and I can't wait to taste you. Sorry, I'm a little drunk and turned on.
Mark: Don't apologize. Me too. I love that!
Julie: God, I can't wait!
Mark: Me too.
Julie: I've started having dreams.
Mark: Am I in them?
Julie: Oh yeah!

I wanted to revel in my sexuality and get caught up in the fantasy world we had created.

When the texting would turn more explicit during the evenings, I would excuse myself and continue in private. Andrew was either uninterested or ignorant of what was going on. Whichever the case, his lack of concern drove me harder and quicker into Mark's digital arms.

Mark: Thinking about you.
Julie: Really? Me too.

I could feel myself grinning.

Mark: Like what?
Julie: We are in the shower, and I'm licking the water drops that are rolling down your neck. Following them slowly down your body with my mouth until I get ......

I stopped.

Mark: Wow, don't leave me hanging. I'm dying!
Julie: You'll have to wait to see.

Mark: My turn. I can't wait to have you in my bed wearing nothing but panties. I'll start by massaging you and gliding my hands down to the hollow of your back. Then I'll slide down, kissing you along the way. When I reach the seam of your panties, I will continue to kiss until I get to your... Oh, no. you'll have to wait too.

I giggled.

Julie: Bite me.

Mark: Don't worry. I plan to.

Chapter 36

MARK IS FORTY TOO. Our birthdays are only two months apart. He comes from a small town outside of Philadelphia and grew up in what would be considered an average, all-American family. His dad was a decorated Vietnam Air Force pilot turned successful real estate investor, and his mother was a pediatric nurse. He had an older brother who was a star athlete and a little sister who was the brain. Being the middle child, he was the quintessential underachiever and irresponsible smart-ass.

Mark floundered his way through college, getting by on his charm and his father's bank account. After graduation, he tried his hand at pharmaceutical sales, high-end car sales, and even tried being a golf pro. He failed miserably at each endeavor, but not all his experiences left him unchanged.

While at the country club, he worked in the pro shop to earn a few extra bucks. During his tenure there, he had a conversation with one of his customers. This man had amassed his fortune through mergers and acquisitions. He explained his business's basic workings, and to Mark, the thought of hostile corporate takeovers was appealing. He was intrigued enough to ask if there were any apprenticeships available. Mark managed to bullshit himself right into a multi-million-dollar career.

He started at the bottom, running errands, making copies, and most importantly, listening to his mentor. Mark learned the ins and outs of cultivating relationships. How to win an enemy's trust, find weaknesses by lulling people into a false sense of security and exploiting them for all they were worth.

Within four years, he had worked his way into a position that allowed him to access the world he had been forever trying to enter. Soon, he started to earn more than he could spend.

I'm not sure why Mark wanted to bring me into his life. I can only guess that perhaps he was getting lonely. His world was filled with staff and servants. His social circle consisted of those who were considered the 'nouveau riche.' He'd found himself in a world where parties didn't end. There was seldom a situation where money couldn't provide a solution.

He dated beautiful young girls who threw themselves at him and would do his bidding, whatever it was. He had done it all, but I suppose even that could lose its luster after a while.

At the end of the day, it was him and his son Johnny in an enormous empty house. There was no one to care for him. No one to love him for who he was, not what he had. By the time he ran into me, he was ready to be swept away into the fantasy of an everyday life. He wanted someone to ground him and be a mother to his son.

Our trip was just around the corner. I was somewhat apprehensive. This was different from my affair with Brandon. This could be a game-changer. Mark was trying to sweep me off my feet, and he was doing a damn fine job of it.

Inexplicably, Andrew gave his blessing. I wanted him to stop me and prove he loved me, but he didn't. He even drove me to the airport. We pulled up to the curbside porter in our quintessential suburban minivan with both children in tow. Andrew got out, took my suitcase from the trunk, kissed me, and wished me a safe trip. My heart was broken before I even got on the plane.

I ignored the voice inside my head, screaming for me not to go as I approached the gate. The only way not to live with a lifetime of doubt was to walk onto that plane.

On arrival at Southwest International Airport, my shirt was soaking with sweat, and my hands were clammy. I ducked into the closest bathroom and hid in a stall. "What the hell am I doing?" I began to cry. I knew it was wrong, but it seemed there was no going back. Andrew didn't want me; he never did. I would have to make the best of the trip, reminding myself that this might be my last chance at happiness.

After pulling myself together, I dabbed a drop of perfume behind each ear and one on my belly, raked my fingers through my hair, and freshened up my makeup. Ready or not, here I come.

As promised, a driver was waiting for me with my name on a white sign written in black ink. We walked to the car making small talk. We spoke about the weather and traffic at that time of day. As Jeffery, the driver, and I continued our conversation, I realized that I was continually referring to my husband and children.

"So, Jeffery, do you have any children?"

"Yes, ma'am, I have a boy and a girl."

"Me too," I said. "My boy is the sweetest thing, and my daughter, God, do I love her, but she sure knows how to push my buttons. My husband calls her a terrorist without a cause."

"Mine is that way too. That's girls for you," he smiled in commiseration in the rear-view mirror.

"My husband has little patience for her. It's funny how riled she can get him. Secretly, I find it hysterical. She is a good girl, but..." I lifted a single brow.

I wondered if it was apparent that I was there to have an affair. Did I look guilty?

While in the car, Mark called. I contemplated not answering it. We had spoken only two or three times in total. The thought of talking to him made me uncomfortable. I liked hiding behind my written words. I didn't want him to see me. I didn't want him to know that I was not perfect.

"Hello?"

"Hey, you! How far away are you?" his voice gave away his eagerness.

"Not sure. I got stuck at the gate, and now we're in traffic."

"Oh, come on! Hurry up and get here.

"I'm trying. What are you doing?"

"Drinking a beer, looking at the water."

"Oh, you stink. I've got to tell you; I'm really nervous."

"I knew you would be. Did you have a glass of wine on the plane?"

"No. I didn't want to get tired. Oh, my goodness, Jeffrey just told me we are only five minutes away. Are you sure you still want me to come? You can back out," I offered.

"Are you kidding? It's all I have thought about for weeks."

"Okay. If you're sure, I'll be there shortly. Bye." I hung up, wondering if this was a huge mistake.

The car turned right between two massive iron gates and proceeded up a long gravel driveway. A stately white, Spanish-inspired villa came into view. The property was neatly manicured with lush tropical plantings thoughtfully grouped. As we got closer, a massive walnut door opened, and there he stood. Afraid to let my eyes linger one place too long, I looked at Jeffery to thank him. Opening the car door, Mark took my hand to help me out. In front of me stood my future lover. The man I had been dating but with whom I had never had an actual date. We reached for each other and hugged in an awkward embrace. Mark paid for the driver, took my suitcase, and ushered me into a grand foyer.

We stood staring at each other, not knowing what to do next. We laughed, trying to diffuse the unease. He took my hand. "Come on, I want to show you around."

The patio doors were wide open, and all my senses filled at once with the smell, sight, and sound of the gulf was everywhere. He smiled at my reaction. He had hoped I would be pleased.

Turning to my host, boyfriend, and lover, "Here," I said and handed him a bottle of champagne I had brought. "Thank you for having me."

"Thank you for coming. Let's go into the kitchen and open it."

As we entered the room, I could see that all the design elements were top of the line. He grabbed two champagne flutes, Baccarat, of course, and poured us both a glass. Lifting his glass to make a toast, "Here's to old acquaintances becoming new friends." We clinked, and he gave me a guided tour.

He beamed with pride as we visited each room. I admired the molding, the columns, the bookshelves, and the marble. The house boasted six bedrooms, seven bathrooms, a library, a formal living room, dining room, family room, game room, state-of-the-art gym, and, of course, the gourmet kitchen. Floating from one room to the next, I was in awe. I had read in magazines he was wealthy but had no idea the extent.

"You're the first woman I have invited here."

"Really? Well, in that case, I am truly flattered."

We stood looking at each other, smiling uncomfortably, not knowing what to do next. The tension was mounting. I had to kiss him. Every second that passed was a second too long. I stepped forward and touched his hair, stood on my tippy toes, and leaned up, tilting my head slightly and gently placing my parted lips on his. He met my mouth with his, and our tongues explored the new territory. The rush of a first kiss exploded inside me, and I surrendered to the moment. It was as if I was letting out a breath I had held in for too long. I looked at him and giggled as if a young schoolgirl. As much as I enjoyed the kiss, I knew it wasn't magic. I think he did, too.

Chapter 37

MARK AND I SPENT the next few hours looking at the water as boats were gliding past. We sipped champagne and talked about how our lives had unfolded and the circumstances that brought us together. I don't think either of us was willing to give up on the fantasy we had spent months building. Not after one so so kiss.

I stood with my glass in hand and walked closer to the water to watch the sunset. He came behind and began to play with my hair. My head naturally moved into him.

"I bought a vineyard in Napa six months ago; I would love to show it to you sometime. I thought we could go there for a weekend. Would you like that?"

"Maybe," I purred, feeling lulled by his stroking. Perhaps I was too hasty in judging the situation after just one kiss. I am never sure what part of myself to trust.

Time flew quickly, and it was almost eight o'clock in the evening. "I made nine o'clock reservations at this little authentic Japanese restaurant. Hurry up and get ready," he fretted.

"We don't have to go out. I'm enjoying being here. Why don't we order in and just hang out?" I wanted to understand who this person was that had cast a spell so strong that it pulled me to Florida and away from my family.

"I want to take you out and show you off. Come on." He said with a slight pout on his lips that was irresistible.

He guided me through his cavernous bedroom to a massive bathroom with monogrammed towels and a marble shower. He drew me close to him, trapping me in a kiss, and began to remove my clothing. I reached for his and did the same. We purposefully and methodically undressed each other with a delicious seductiveness that made us both sigh deeply. Our bodies craving to be touched. He walked over and ran a warm shower that we both entered. The water ran down my body as he lathered my back and kissed the nape of my neck. My back arched when he reached around to the front and cupped my breasts in his hands. He turned me around and backed me up against the wall, and I let out a scream as the chill of the marble electrified my warm, naked body. My screech broke the spell.

We stood before the mirror, drying off. I asked him if I could have some privacy; instead of being agreeable, I saw something in his demeanor change. That was the first time I noticed my presence in his space was beginning to make him uneasy.

We arrived at the restaurant in his black Mercedes SLK55. We were shown to a secluded table in the far back, where a bottle of Saki awaited us. We lifted our glasses and made a toast to the weekend and to the future, whatever may happen. With each sip, my inhibition lessened. I was living out a fantasy. Leaning over, I kissed him and placed my hand on his thigh.

When dinner was over, our passions were stirring powerfully. We forwent dessert and returned to his house. The excitement that had been building up for the last few months became more intense over the last few hours and exploded as we walked in the door. It wasn't long before our kisses turned more passionate and frantic. We tore at each other's clothes, ripping off everything with complete disregard for buttons or hooks. He laid me down on the couch and touched me. His hands met with every part of my flesh. My knees were weak, and my self-control weaker. He knelt at the edge of the couch and took me in his mouth. He stayed there until I let out a soft moan of satisfaction. With that, he continued until he felt my rigid body go limp. Mark came up and kissed me again. Tasting myself on his lips caused a renewing of my passion. We were both eager. He parted my legs and slipped inside. Every neuron was emitting pulses of electricity; I was swept away in the current.

I wish I could call what Mark and I did "making love," but it wasn't. We had sex. Hot, steamy, and wild sex. When it was over, he got up, grabbed a cigarette and a beer, and went outside to the veranda, not even glancing my way.

I laid naked on the couch, trying to figure out what had just happened. Why had he walked away? I heard no more sweet talk or fantasies of us being together. Was I once again playing the fool? Had my search for love blinded me from the truth? Perhaps it was simple. He got what he had set out for, and no longer had use for me. I was another one of his hostile takeovers. Much as he did in business, he read me, got me to trust him, and went in for the kill.

The truth was chasing me, and my self-loathing was nipping at my heels, but I was going to outrun it. I tried to rid myself of romantic notions gone awry and salvage some of my pride. His shirt hung over a chair, so I slipped it on, leaving it unbuttoned, exposing a peek of my tight yoga body. Walking over, I grabbed the cigarette he held between his fingers. I took a long drag, ran my fingers through his hair, and returned inside to wash up for bed. I figured if I played it cool, he wouldn't know how his behavior was affecting me. The show must go on.

Following me in, he invited me to sleep next to him, and I took him up on his offer. I crawled in, ready for us to hold each other as lovers do. Instead, he gave me a quick kiss, grabbed his pillow, and held it instead.

Eventually, I fell asleep with the help of a sleeping pill. I woke at five-thirty. Not wanting to wake him, I snuck out of the room to call Danni. I went out on the balcony with my cell phone and dialed my lifeline. As I waited for her to answer, I was lulled by the ebb and flow over the rocky shoreline. There is still such beauty in the world, I reminded myself. Then she answered.

"How's it going? Is he hot and juicy? What is his place like? Did you do it?" Her succession of questions was shot at me like bullets.

"It's really awkward. It's like waking up with a guy you hardly know after a night of drinking, only worse. It's as if he's sorry that I'm here. Shit! I think I fucked up again."

"Well, how was it?" Her voice sang the question.

"It was okay. He acted peculiar afterward. But let's forget about him for now. You should see this house. It is unbelievable!" We laughed the same way we did in high school the morning after one of us had a big date. The call wound down when her baby started to cry for her breakfast.

She left me with this one final comment, "Be careful and don't get hurt!"

"Don't worry so much about me," I said. "I'm perfectly capable of taking care of myself." But in my head, I replied sadly, *too late*.

We hung up, and I sat curled up on the plush outdoor couch—the stink of the full ashtray wafted up my nose, a sharp reminder of the night before. I walked over to the sliding door and found myself smiling as I stared at him sleeping. The white sheets were wrapped around his torso, exposing his muscular hairless chest. His physicality drew me in, leaving commonsense to vanish. Removing my t-shirt, I crawled into bed with him.

He awoke slowly, opening one eye and then the other. I gave him my famous half-smile with a not-so-secret meaning.

"Morning," he grumbled.

"Morning, sleepyhead," I responded in my most seductive voice.

"Hey, can you make some coffee?" He said between yawns.

"Sure thing." I'm not sure what I was expecting.

Leaving him to his own devices, I wandered into the magnificent kitchen to brew up a pot, but after a thorough search, none was to be found. Upon my return, he was up and dressed with his car keys in hand. "Let's go grab some breakfast."

We drove in silence to a small coffee shop that didn't look like much from the outside. The name outside read "Heavenly Biscuits," and the smell of the homemade cinnamon rolls and freshly brewed coffee was, in fact, Heaven.

After consuming a biscuit and half a cup of hazelnut vanilla coffee, he uttered his first words since we left. "Sorry, I guess I woke up a little cranky."

"Boy, you would think we were an old married couple." I laughed at his detachment.

His glare told me all his words didn't say. The alarm bells that had been ringing in my head for the last couple of months went into high gear. It was as if I put my life on a railroad track, and a train was bearing down on me. The whistles blew, the bell dinged, and even the black and white arm came down, but I still ignored them all. I hoped there was a way we were able to save the weekend. I wanted so badly for everything to work out. I thought, Please, Mark, give me one glimmer of hope. Please don't be a jerk. Please don't let me have been so wrong again.

He looked at my plate and, seeing I had barely touched my breakfast, said, "You don't eat much, do you? What, are you on a diet or something?"

"I'm feeling a little cranky." I couldn't resist poking fun at his earlier comment.

I tried to make a lighthearted conversation, but he appeared sullen and withdrawn. I wasn't sure how to handle it since I barely knew him. I decided to take action. When we were done eating, I announced that I wanted to go shopping and buy a new dress for the evening's dinner. I figured, what the hell? The day wasn't going to be a total bust. Surprisingly, he was in complete agreement. After settling the check, we were off to find me the perfect ensemble.

We glided down Fifth Avenue in downtown Naples. Everywhere there were small boutiques with gorgeous clothing displayed in the windows. I spotted a kimono-style sheath in the window of one such store. Ducking inside to get a better look, I noticed the price tag: $1,100.00. Following me, he held the silky garment between his hands, letting it dance between his fingers.

Before I had a chance to say anything, a small, dark-haired Israeli woman approached us. "You have exquisite taste." She nodded in the direction of the dress and then at me. "If I may be so bold, I think it is just her size."

"Yes," he said. "I think so."

I was ushered to a small white room with satin draping. I wondered what that woman was thinking. Did she wonder if I was his wife? His lover? Probably not. Only one other word came to mind, but I pushed it out of my head. "Who cares what she thinks?" I said aloud and shook my head as if to physically remove the dreaded word from my brain.

"Excuse me, Miss. Your gentleman friend would like to see this on you as well."

"Thank you." I said, taking the items from her extended hands, "I'll be right out." I put on the strappy pair of champagne-colored sandals, held the pearl-skinned leather handbag, and wore the gold beaded necklace. The outfit was now complete.

I walked back into the store, where Mark waited for me. "You clean up nicely."

Was that meant to be a compliment?

Oddly, it was reminiscent of the shopping sprees I had with my grandmother as a little girl.

It was then; that I realized it was likely that he finds happiness in the power his money affords him. He still had to learn what I already knew. Whether sexual or financial, power is often fleeting, but I would let him have his moment.

As the day progressed, I tried to give him space, but it was difficult under the circumstances. I was able to see the level of intimacy we were sharing was hurting him. Real relationships cannot be achieved with texting; therefore, he didn't realize how uncomfortable our real-life romance would make him.

Perhaps my marriage was no longer an abstract concept. Possibly he came to understand that I was putting everything on the line for him, for us, and it freaked him out. His discomfort only served to make mine worse.

We spent the rest of the afternoon lounging by the pool, drinking Bellini's. When he went inside to make a phone call, I called Danni on the verge of tears. I worked hard to put up the illusion of being relaxed, but I hated what was happening in reality.

"Hey, got a minute?" I asked.

"Sure, Jul. What's the matter?"

"This is a disaster. I don't know what to do. God, I'm such an idiot! I don't understand why he is so different from the guy I got to know over the last couple of months."

"Hon, that's just the point. You don't know him, and you are not an idiot. You are a romantic, and there's nothing wrong with that. He told you what he wanted you to hear. I'm so sorry this is happening to you. I was hoping that he would be everything you had been dreaming of. Jul, he's the idiot if he doesn't see that you are the best thing to ever happen to him. He's damn lucky you even gave him the time of day," she added sympathetically. "Don't let him do this to you. You're amazing. He's the asshole. Be strong. I love you so much."

"I'll try to be, but no promises. Love you too. Talk to you later." I snapped my phone shut, wiping away the remnants of my tears. I had been sitting with my back to the doorway when we ended the call and didn't see Mark had returned.

He must have caught the tail end of the conversation, "What does that mean?" he seemed inordinately concerned that I may have been discussing him or, at the very least, my visit, which of course, I was.

"What?" I said, pretending I had no idea what he was referring to.

"When you said, 'you'd try to be."

"Oh, I was just saying I would try to be awake enough to call her when I got home."

I stood and kissed him long and hard, hoping that I would be able to hide my sadness behind physical affection, precisely as I always have.

Chapter 38

AN INTERESTING THING ABOUT Mark and me is that we are similar in some ways. We are both funny and sensitive, enjoy home and family, and are both insecure. He would probably never admit to the latter, but it's true. In trying to identify the problem further, I now realize most of our conversations revolved around stories of what he was building, buying, or doing. Whom he knew, and where he was going? Nothing of what he was sharing was real. I don't think he liked to recognize there was someone inside of him who could be endearing, funny, loving, and sensitive. That would have made him too vulnerable. I caught a glimpse of that part of him before our weekend. It was why I had fallen for him. Unfortunately, that part of him didn't make this trip.

His financial success is the full measure of his self-worth. I know a lot about what he is doing because I have done something similar. The difference, I use my sexuality and my body instead of money. Both of our insecurities were emerging. We were trying to convince ourselves we were worthy of attention, worthy of being loved.

In the last twenty-four hours, I have had many feelings for Mark. I certainly felt a passion, physical lust, disappointment, and anger. Now I feel sadness and empathy. The longer I stayed with him, the better I began to understand him. He was no longer hiding behind the phone he always carried with him. He had to show his eyes; he could no longer hide his soul. Perhaps it was my responsibility to help him evolve and grow past the superficial existence he was living. I couldn't desert him now.

That evening, we were going out for dinner again. When we sat, I ordered a Manhattan before looking at the menu. I was wearing the dress, shoes, purse, and necklace he bought me, but he sat across the table, not looking at me but rather through me. Instead of living out a dream, I was caught in a nightmare. I wonder if he thought he had bought me. If so, he was mistaken. I was not for sale at any price. I ordered a second drink.

We ordered our food and sat in silence, waiting for it to arrive. While picking at our appetizers, Mark asked, "Are you going to tell Andrew we slept together?"

"I haven't decided. There are many things to consider," I quipped as I nonchalantly played with my food.

He was quick to snap at me, "Don't! I don't want to be a part of it."

I was stunned by the force of his proclamation. He had chased me, knowing I was married. He had continued to seduce me when I exposed my vulnerabilities. This man lured me away from my husband and children with the implications of a happily ever after. It wasn't all him. I was indeed a willing participant. I went into this with the full knowledge of what I was doing. I accepted the possible consequences, but he was in the thick of it regardless of whether Andrew would find out.

That was when his true colors began to shine through.

"What the fuck, Julie? There is no reason to say anything."

"Perhaps not for you, but there is for me. Anyway, who do you think you are ordering me around?"

He quickly asked for the check before our entrees arrived and escorted me out.

He did not open the car door for me or look at me. The engine revved loud enough to turn heads as we sped out of the driveway.

Upon our return, he went directly to his office, and I went outside, where the sand was cold, and the moon was reflecting off the water. While watching the stars glitter in the sky, I wondered if, after all the years of having what he wanted on his terms, did he have any sense of empathy or accountability? After an hour, I went to bed. Alone. I have no idea where he spent the night, but it wasn't in his room.

I realize now that there are certain things I have taken for granted in my relationship with Andrew. The freedom to say anything without analyzing each word or always wondering if everything is my fault. The relinquishing of personal space and sharing everything and anything. I have eaten off my husband's plate, drank out of my son's glass, and shared the same fork with my daughter without giving it a second thought. It is a way of life. It's a family.

I don't want to do this.

In the morning, Mark found me packing.

"Sorry about last night. I feel shitty about everything that went on," he said.

"You should."

"I think I took advantage of you. This was all too much," his eyes pleaded with me to be understanding.

"I am a grown woman and came into this with my eyes wide open," I tried to relieve him of his guilt. I'm not sure why. I suppose because I didn't want him to feel as badly as I did.

I would be leaving Naples in a few short hours, and I thought about how much I missed my children. I missed tucking them in bed, singing our songs, and saying our prayers. I missed hearing Tess sing her baby dolls to sleep and helping Jack read a book. I missed the comfort of my house, knowing the people around me loved me and wanted me there. It was time for me to go home.

I did my best to be friendly and outgoing during breakfast. Although not what I had hoped, our time together did bring with it a certain clarity. I learned that I still wasn't able to trust anyone, no matter what they say. That some people never change, and there are certain things about myself that I still don't like.

I suppose some women would feel lucky or grateful to have an experience such as the one I had.

To be swept into a world the average person didn't see, even for a short time. I was bombarded by many emotions, but lucky and grateful weren't the adjectives I would use.

We sat on the beach, waiting for the clock to tick down. Our relationship had been text-based for the same reasons Andrew got lost in the world of cyber-porn. It was a safe place to hide. Mark didn't notice I had left to collect the remainder of my belongings.

His housekeeper, Marta, was in the primary bedroom changing the linens when I came in. I was hesitant to enter, not knowing the protocol.

"It's all right to come in. I'm almost done."

I took the opportunity to ask a couple of questions.

"How do you like working here?"

"Mr. Sullivan is a wonderful man. He takes very good care of me and my family."

"How long have you worked for him?"

"Fifteen years now. I'm lucky to have such a wonderful employer."

"Well, it was lovely to meet you," I said as I extended my hand to shake hers.

"Thank you. Nice meeting you too. I'll see you again soon, no?"

"I don't think so. Take care," My voice trailed off.

I put my bags by the front door and joined Mark by the pool. He had a bottle of Louis Roederer Cristal chilling in a silver wine bucket with two glasses waiting. I gulped the first glass down and poured another. I hadn't set out to get drunk, but suddenly I couldn't resist.

"You know," I said, speaking with the boldness the champagne gave me, "I don't think you're ready to have a woman in your life."

"You're right. I'm not. Besides, I hate drama!" I wasn't able to contain the giggle that bubbled up. After all, the entire situation was dramatic from start to finish.

Only fifteen minutes until the car would arrive. I prayed for it to pass quickly.

By the time my ride came down the driveway, I was drunk and kissed him one final time. I did so, knowing my great love affair was a complete failure. It would be our last kiss, and probably the last time I would see him ever again. The driver loaded my bag into the trunk as I entered the car. When we pulled away, neither of us looked back.

The airport bar was packed, but I found an empty stool tucked into the corner. "Martini, please," I mouthed to the bartender. I took out my phone in a one ditch effort to salvage my pride. I hoped Mark and I could return to being friends. Then everything wouldn't be quite so bad. Every few seconds, I checked my phone, and no new alerts appeared. I tried it again—still, no response. Before our departure, I ordered two more drinks. I sank back into my leather seat and pulled the stiff blue airline blanket over my head. I wished I could take the last three days back, but that was not going to happen. I had no Superman to spin the world in the opposite direction to turn back time. God damn it, this can't be happening.

Upon my arrival at Newark, I was greeted by my two beautiful children and my husband, who loved me. Who shared my life, my bathroom, and would share my bed happily if I would let him. The husband who, I realized at that moment, I didn't love. I had failed at my marriage and my love affairs. I was a three-time loser. The words failure, loser, bitch, adulteress, whore, stupid, and ugly went around and around in my head. I deserved every horrible thing I felt.

Chapter 39

ONCE WE WERE HOME, we got the children settled in bed. I snuggled up close to them, feeling their breath grow calm as they drifted off to sleep.

I climbed into my bed with my head throbbing from the alcohol and the emotional overload. I don't think I said more than a word or two since we had walked in the door. Andrew came into my room and asked if I would allow him to spend the night with me. I answered, "Sure," because it didn't matter to me. Nothing mattered. He was asleep in moments, and I cried into my pillow all night. It hurt for me to breathe. It hurt to be alive. I silently screamed and berated myself for always being stupid and weak. All the pain I had spent my life denying was coming up full force, and I was unable to suppress it anymore. The black hole I had always struggled against was swallowing me up. I was disappearing into misery.

The morning came too quickly. I crawled out of bed hungover, only to be faced with having to spend the day with Andrew's family. I wanted to stay in bed with the sheets pulled up over my head. It was impossible to hide my despair and shame. The darkness inside would undoubtedly follow me around and be seen by all. I pulled myself together and tried to convince the world around me that I was in control. Andrew realized that something monumental had to have happened. He knew me better than anyone else in the world.

I did my job playing the dutiful wife. I helped prepare the meal, serve the food, pour wine, and make small talk. I giggled at stories I didn't find funny and kept a pasted smile on my face for as long as possible. The charade continued for hours until I no longer had the fortitude to go on. I was sitting at the table when I got dizzy, and the world started to fade. Andrew saw the blood run out of my face and the unfocused look in my eyes. He grabbed my hand and led me outside, where he hoped the cool air would bring me around. He walked me up the street, supporting me with every step. I decided I had to tell him everything.

"I slept with Mark. I cheated on you. I'm so sorry. I don't know what else to say." The words hung in the air.

"You could start with why you did it."

"I'm tired of hurting. I don't have any fight left, and you didn't stop me." I gulped at the air as if water. "I know you don't care what I'm doing as long as it doesn't interfere with your life. You knew what was going to happen, and you let it." I cried.

"I know I don't show how I feel the way I should, and I should have told you not to go. I fucked up."

He looked angrier with himself than with me. "It was stupid, but I love you, and I don't want you to be with anyone else. We both have made some huge mistakes, but we can get past this. I know we can," he said, holding my hands. I trembled, and I think he understood whatever anger or sadness he had at that moment paled in comparison to what I was going through. Of course, he was angry with Mark and me, but also with himself. He shared in the blame. "No, I didn't stop you, but I didn't say have sex with him, either. Let's get that straight. I shouldn't have let you go, but I didn't want you to get mad at me. God, this is all so messed up. I never know the right thing to do."

Perhaps I should have been thankful that he was so forgiving, but instead, I was confused. I heard the words that he loved me and forgave me, but somehow it didn't fit. He wasn't angry or jealous. He acted oddly relieved. As if now, everything was going to be okay because we were on an equal playing field. We had both nearly destroyed our marriage, and it seemed in his mind that we should be able to move on. But I couldn't forgive him that easily or, for that matter, myself.

I thought unburdening myself with the truth would release me, but it didn't. The last several years had turned me into someone unrecognizable.

Andrew took me to the car and gathered the children, telling his family I was sick, which wasn't far from the truth.

Once home, he led me to the couch when we got home. I was paralyzed by grief. For hours I stared as a small black spider outside the window worked on its web. It released the silk from its body, weaving an intricate design that would later catch her prey. Was I the spider or the prey?

The weekend came and went. I was lost in the pain that consumed me. From time to time, unstoppable tears would stream down my face. They weren't accompanied by sobs or loud cries, only endless rivers of tears.

"Julie, can you hear me?" I was unable to answer. The void that was once only a small part of my heart had engulfed me.

"Jul, I'm taking the week off. I will take care of the kids. You rest."

He took the children to school, and while he was gone, I went to the kitchen to call the one person who might be able to help me, Laura.

When I got to her office, she stood at the top of the stairs to greet me and shuffled me directly into her room.

"What's going on?" She was noticeably shocked by my matted hair and stained clothing.

"Oh, god, I don't even know where to start."

"Start with what happened to put you in this state. You were in fairly good shape last we spoke."

"Mark, the one I thought might be the answer to my prayers, only wanted to fuck me." I laughed a laugh that was not at all funny. "Big surprise there. Laura, why do all men only want to fuck me? Well, everyone except my husband. Talk about Murphy's Law." I shook my head. "Ever since I was a little girl, it's always been about fucking me. I don't understand it. Why would anyone want to hurt a little girl? Why would anyone want to take advantage of another human being? What have I done to deserve this? Why are people so mean?" I began to cry harder. "Laura, I am so angry with myself. I can't believe I was this stupid again. How could I have possibly believed him? I thought he was my friend. I'm such an idiot!" I covered my face in an attempt to hide. "My mother was right; I am stupid. I was a stupid little girl who turned into a stupid woman. Jesus Christ, what the hell is wrong with me?"

"Stop beating yourself up. You are not stupid; you are human. You are allowed to make mistakes. Let's take one step at a time. Did you think he was your friend?"

"Yes. I had no reason to doubt it. I thought he genuinely cared about me. I cared about him."

"What do you actually know about him?"

"I knew the person he used to be. I didn't like him in college, but I honestly thought he had changed. People can change, can't they?"

"Did he?" Her face was deadpanned.

"No. Not at all."

"Let's talk about why you had this affair and what makes it different from what happened with Brandon," she said.

"I went to Naples because I wanted to find happiness. I wanted to be loved, taken care of, and protected. I'm tired of being treated like crap by everyone." I crossed my legs in a double knot.

"You have said several times in the past and again now that you want to be loved and treated well. But you're not doing any of that."

"I'm not doing any of what?" I didn't comprehend what she was trying to say.

Laura moved forward and lowered her voice. "Julie, this behavior is you punishing yourself for something you had no control over. Before fully loving another, you need to learn self-love and self-care."

I hate myself. I always have. Maybe I do treat myself like crap because—well, I don't know why. I guess because I deserve it. Did I deserve what happened to me at age nine, eleven, or seventeen? God, I just want it all to go away. I'm still that same little girl hiding in my closet, crying for hours. I don't want to cry anymore.

"Let me ask you. Have you contacted Mark since you got back?" asked Laura.

"I've tried several times, but he won't respond."

"What do you hope to accomplish by speaking with him?"

"I just want the truth. I want to know why he did this. I so badly wanted him to care, but he didn't, not at all. I found out yesterday that he is getting married. How fucked up is that? He was engaged to some twenty-five-year-old blonde when I went. This was all a game to him," I laughed in disgust.

"Do you want to marry him? Are you willing to break up your family for him?"

"Absolutely not! I'm not even sure I like him as a human being, but I did want to be more than just his whore. I'm not a whore!" I said, pleading for her to believe me and trying to convince myself simultaneously.

"No, you're not, and you should remember that. Who is it you are trying to convince? Him or You?"

"Both," I mumbled quietly.

"You need to remember that you are a valuable woman. You have so much more to offer than your body. You are funny, bright, and perceptive. I want you to see yourself the way the rest of the world does. You need to start respecting yourself. This Mark character seems to be symbolic of your past. He is a representation of all the men who made you feel like a whore. You are fighting a ghost. You need to stop."

"Okay, how do I do that?" I prayed, hoping she would have a quick fix.

"It's time for you to look at everything you have buried. You keep putting off all the things you don't want to deal with. It's time for you to make peace with yourself." She made it sound so easy.

"So, where do we start?" I wondered aloud.

"Let's start with what happened to the men who abused you. Did you ever see them again?"

I closed my eyes, trying to find the courage to begin. I never wanted to have to say their names again. "Jerry disappeared after a while. Honestly, I don't know what happened to him. I have whole chunks of time from around then that I don't remember." Pressing my fingers to my temples, trying to rub away the throbbing, I said, "My mom's friend Barry came around from time to time. I usually hid in my room whenever he was over. Do you want to hear something funny?"

Laura nodded.

"Two years ago, Jackie called me crying because he'd had a stroke and died."

"What did you say to that?" Laura raised a single eyebrow.

"I said, good, I hope he rots in hell. Mom said, 'Stop that, Julie. He was my friend, and I'm sad he is gone. I'm going to miss him.' Can you believe that? She was mourning that child molester. The man deserved to be in jail. God only knows how many other children he molested," I said in disgust. "For God's sake, the man had his own children." The room was quiet for a moment, and then I asked, "Laura, why won't this all go away? Why can't I get over it? It was so long ago. It doesn't matter anymore."

"That is where you are wrong. It matters just as much now as it did back then. Abuse is not something you can get over. It is a part of you. It is ingrained in your psyche. Everyone is a product of an accumulation of experiences. Some experience a supportive family environment and unconditional love from mothers and fathers. Some aren't so lucky and experience neglect and abuse. Most people land somewhere in the middle. Regardless, we all experience a certain amount of dysfunction in our lives. That dysfunction or lack thereof plays a major role in determining who we are and how we process our thoughts. You will never get over it, and you are unable to change it. But you can make peace with it and quiet its voice. It's finally time to start doing that. Are you ready?"

"I really don't know. One thing is for sure, I'm terrified. I don't want to go back there." Without noticing, I shredded the tissue in my hand, leaving specks of white everywhere.

"It can be scary, but we will do it together. I promise we will work through this, and you will finally be able to find some peace. True peace. No more running away from it, okay?" Laura's voice was soft and convincing.

"Okay," I said, wiping the tears from my eyes.

"You are doing great, Julie. I'm proud of you for calling. You are much stronger than you give yourself credit for. Remember, we are doing this together." She handed me a small piece of paper. "Here is a prescription for Xanax. If you feel like you're sinking, take a half and go to sleep. This will take a while, and you'll need to be patient, but I am here for you. I am only a phone call away."

I stood with the prescription in my hand. "Thanks for not saying I deserve everything I got and not calling me a whore. I mean, about the affairs and all."

"I would never do that, Julie. You are not a whore. I know this unequivocally. I know you. You are many things, but that word is nothing but a preconceived notion someone put in your head a long time ago. It does not define you." As I stood to leave, she said, "Nothing you say or do will ever scare me away. You are safe here." Safe. That was a concept I was completely unfamiliar with.

I looked at the paper she held and made an appointment for the following Friday morning at ten. On my way home, I stopped at the drug store to fill the prescription and renew my Ambien script.

By the time I got home, Andrew was waiting for me. "Where the hell have you been?" he demanded.

"I went to see Laura. I'm falling apart. She gave me some Xanax. Yeah, now I'm on antidepressants. God, I'm such a loser."

"You're not a loser. You're just dealing with a lot. No thanks to me," he said sadly.

"I'm going to take these and go to bed. I need you to handle things around here for a while. Do you think you can do that?"

"I'll do whatever you want. I'm going to take the rest of the week, no, the next two weeks off. I have a lot of vacation coming my way. You stay in bed and rest. I'm sure you're exhausted. I'll handle everything."

"Thanks," I said over my shoulder, leaving the room.

One day rolled into the next. I rarely left my room. I sat in bed, analyzing who I had once been, who I had become, and how I had gotten so lost. I couldn't let go of the past and start living in the present. I broke down every part of the last forty years. Every action and reaction. I desperately wanted to make sense of anything and everything.

The following Thursday, Jack had his first baseball game. "Hey, honey. Why don't you get up, take a warm shower, and come to Jack's game? It would make him so happy," Andrew said, trying to entice me.

"No," I said sharply. "I can't stand sitting around with all those cackling bitches. God, I hate them! They all look at me as if I'm a weirdo, anyway. It's like I have some fucking scarlet letter on my chest. I'm not going to pretend to be one of them." I threw the pillow over my head to hide. I hated everyone and everything. Our house, our town, his clothes, our lives. I hated it all. I wasn't even sure how I felt about my children. With that thought, I started to cry again.

Andrew sat on the bed and stroked my arm to calm me down. "Stop that!" I barked at him. "I hate when you do that. It's so God damn annoying."

"Sorry, honey. Everything is going to be okay. I'll videotape it, and we'll watch it together later," he said sweetly.

"Okay. I'm sorry I've turned into a freak show," I cried.

"It's okay. Try not to worry so much. Everything is going to work out." I thought his expectations were high, considering my whole life was crumbling around me. I was a stranger who was a complete basket case. He said everything was going to work out. I didn't see how that was possible, considering everything that had happened. Besides, when exactly did he become Mr. Fucking Ray of Sunshine?

I'm sure he was starting to wonder how much longer he would be able to handle what was happening. I was mean, depressed, and, let's face it, downright crazy. It was obvious his compassion and patience were starting to wear thin. Whose wouldn't?

I listened to hear the front door close, and as soon as I did, I went downstairs and filled up a tumbler with vodka and ice. No mixer. That would only delay the desired effect. After my first glass, I took a sleeping pill. I made myself one more drink. Although drowsy, sleep wouldn't come. The images of my life were flashing through my mind like a reel of film. Each ugly mistake I had ever made kept coming.

I was born. Interloper! At age five, I ran into the street after my ball; a car swerved to miss me and hit a telephone pole. It was my fault. Stupid! When I was eight, I played dress-up with Mommy's jewelry and lost her favorite earrings. No wonder she hates me. Irresponsible! At nine, I caused a grown man to molest me. Tease! When I was eleven, Jerry bruised me. Slut! When I was seventeen, I got drunk and let Bobby take the one thing I kept sacred. Whore! By eighteen, I started sleeping around. Tramp! When I was twenty-five, I broke Brian's heart. Bitch! When I was twenty-seven, I married a man who didn't love me. Moron! I lost myself to him. Weak! At thirty-eight, I had an affair. Selfish! When I was forty, I had another, thinking it would save me. Naive! Now I am here. I am the cause of my undoing. I took another sleeping pill. I wanted my mind to Shut up! Shut up! Shut up! Please!!! Shut the fuck up, you stupid, stupid whore.

Everything went dark.

Chapter 40

IT'S NOT ALWAYS EASY being married to Julie. I know I seem like a complete asshole, but I'm not, really. I'm just the opposite of Julie. Well, not entirely, let's just say, emotionally. The first time I saw her, I was drawn to her, as many men are, but I was invisible to her. She gave off an air that told the world that she was strong and incredibly comfortable in her skin. I admired that. Whatever I did to make her notice me must have worked because now she and the children are my family, and God, do I love them, contrary to what she thinks. I never thought in a million years that I would be lucky enough to have a life like the one she has given me or have the love of an incredible woman like her. It kind of scared me for a while.

Julie feels things in a way I can't even understand and does things I could never do. She says she feels with her soul. I have no idea what that means. I guess I would say I feel things with my brain. It would never occur to me to make her a birthday cake or call her during the day to ask how she is, but that doesn't mean I don't love her. I'm not wired that way.

I obviously wasn't thinking when I told her about Paige. I wasn't really in love with her when I married Julie. I loved Julie. I honestly did and still do. What I was trying to say was that I still had unresolved feelings for Paige. It came out wrong. As soon as I saw the pain on her face, I knew it was the biggest mistake of my life.

As for the whole porn thing, I wish it didn't happen. I didn't even realize that it was a problem at first. I didn't understand why it was a big deal until she made it abundantly clear. She has a way of doing that. If nothing else, you always know exactly where you stand with her. She doesn't hold her feelings back and tells you exactly how it is. This can be both a good thing and a bad, depending on the particular topic she is going on and on and on about. She also has a heart as big as Montana, again both good and bad. Good in that she loves big. Bad in that she hurts just as big.

All in all, I'm lucky she chose me. I lost sight of that for a while, but I never will again. I only hope it's not too late.

I need her to snap out of this thing. Seeing her this way is terrifying, but I know she will pull herself out of it. She has to. This mess is mostly my fault. I take full blame. I broke my wife.

It's funny, she has been through so much during her lifetime, and it was me that ultimately pushed her over the edge. I don't even know how it happened. I've got to fix it.

I want to forget about the last few years and get on with our lives. I wish she were able to do that. I don't understand why she can't.

I can't think about this anymore. It's Jack's moment. My boy! My boy is playing baseball. I always wanted to play ball but was too chicken to try out because I was so afraid of failing. He won't have that problem. I'm going to make sure of it. He will never be too scared to try anything.

Wow, he is on fire! At bat six times and hit six times. I'm thrilled, and Tess is so cute cheering for her big brother.

With Tess in my arms, we cheered Jack's team to victory. After an hour and a half, Jack's team had won their first game 6-3. We went out for ice cream to celebrate. It was seven-thirty before we knew it. I needed to get home before Julie started to worry. The kids are both exhausted, and so am I.

"Okay, everyone out of the car and into the house. Hurry up guys, it's late, and it's bedtime."

"We want to say goodnight to Mommy," They both yelled.

"I'm getting there first," Jack started running for the door, strong-arming his sister out of the way.

"No. Not fair. Daddy, make him wait. I want to see Mommy first. Daddy, make him wait!"

We raced up the pathway to the front door. I put my key in, and Jack and Tess pushed past me. They took several steps and stopped dead in their tracks. A look of terror washed over their little faces. I followed their gaze to the landing of the steps. In front of us, Julie was lying at the bottom, her legs twisted underneath her. Her eyes were closed, and her skin was whiter than milk. It took me a second or two to realize that she must have fallen. I ran to her side to check for a pulse. Damn, I couldn't detect anything.

I checked her neck and her wrist. I checked for a hint of air coming from her mouth or nose. I still couldn't tell. The blood in my head rushed so loudly that I could not hear myself think. I began to panic. I still had my cell phone in my pocket and dialed 911. Breathlessly, I began to explain to the dispatcher what had happened.

"Take a deep breath and calm down. I have dispatched the paramedics. They will arrive shortly. Stay on the line. Sir, is she taking any medications?"

"No. Yes! Yes! The doctor gave her a prescription for Xanax this morning, and sometimes she takes a sleeping pill, but ..."

"Sir, do you know if she has been drinking?"

Only then did I notice the strong scent of alcohol on Julie's clothes and skin. In horror, I replied in an almost inaudible voice.

"Oh my God, yes, I think so."

I lifted Julie's limp body, held her in my arms, and rocked her as if she were a baby, just as she had always wanted me to rock our children when they were infants. The tears running down my face landed on hers, making it look like she was crying too.

I started quietly pleading with her, "Please don't leave me. Not now. Not after everything we have been through. You can't." She didn't respond; my voice grew angry. "Goddamn it. You have no right to do this. You can't stop fighting now! You wanted me back, and here I am. For God's sake, open your eyes! Come on! You can't quit now!" I was weeping uncontrollably and screaming at her simultaneously.

What felt like hours but was probably only minutes later, the paramedics came rushing through the door with their medical kits, oxygen, and a stretcher. They moved me aside to attend to her and begin the necessary assessments. I backed away from Julie and grabbed hold of the children, who were crying and holding each other in the corner of the living room. I tried to whisper assuring words, "It's okay. Mommy is going to be fine. She just got a boo-boo." But I don't think I was convincing.

I waited for the paramedics to tell me if she was still alive. I clung to the children for dear life, one under each arm. They held on to me like koalas and buried their heads in my shoulders. The only thought going through my head was, please don't be dead. Jack and Tess need their mommy, and so do I.

The larger of the two paramedics spoke, "Sir, your wife is critical, and we have got to get to the hospital. Follow us in your car."

I piled the children back into the minivan and raced behind the ambulance, careening down our usually quiet street.

Julie was taken into the emergency room and through a pair of white swinging doors. They wouldn't let me in, and I had both children crying in fear. I heard orders being barked and looked on in disbelief as the medical staff flew in and out of the same swinging doors that she had disappeared behind, but had no idea what was happening.

As I sat waiting, the children finally fell asleep on the hard metal chairs. I called Sarah, Julie's sister, and explained what was happening.

Several hours later, she arrived in a grey pair of sweatpants and an oversized dingy Harley Davidson t-shirt, which obviously belonged to someone else.

We each carried one child and placed them back in the car. Before pulling away, she whispered, "Don't worry about them. I'll stay all night, but Andrew, don't let anything happen to her. Promise me!"

"I promise," I said, knowing I had no control over the situation. When she drove away, I had never been more alone in my life than I was at that exact moment.

Two hours had passed when the attending physician came out of the swinging doors with an unreadable face. "Hello. I'm Dr. Simon," he said, extending his hand.

I was wound so tightly that I jumped up like a Jack-in-the-box when the doctor approached. "Hi. How is Julie?"

"Your wife had Xanax, sleeping pills, and alcohol in her system. Was she suicidal?" His approach was direct, without intonation of judgment.

"No, I don't think so. Do you think that was what she was trying to do?" I scratched at my hair.

"Actually, I don't. There wasn't enough to kill her, but certainly enough to disorient her. We pumped her stomach and neutralized the remaining drugs in her system."

"Thank God! She's going to be all right." I let out an enormous sigh of relief and smiled.

"I didn't say that. She has what is called a TBI, a traumatic brain injury. The fall caused swelling around her brain. This is an extremely grave condition. If the pressure is not relieved quickly, she will most certainly have permanent brain damage and possibly die. Mr. Russo, the surgery is not without risk. Many factors are working against us. We will do our best to save your wife; however, her pregnancy will almost certainly be terminated in the process."

"Pregnant? That's not possible." Perhaps I was confused, and I didn't hear him correctly. It was all too much information.

The doctor placed his hand on my shoulder and said, "Mr. Russo, there is no time. I need permission to send Julie to surgery. The O.R. is waiting."

I tried to focus on his face and speak, but was unable to find words.

"Mr. Russo, Andrew, get it together. The longer we wait, the more at risk she is. Your wife needs you now." The Doctor stated firmly.

I chuckled absentmindedly, finding the statement funny, considering who he was talking to. I never had to keep it together in my life. In fact, I don't think I have ever had it apart.

Looking up, I felt a calm wash over me. It was as if I was able to sense Julie's presence. Feeling her love wrapping around me gave me the strength to sign the consent form. It may sound bizarre, and I am far from the ethereal believer. That's Julie's thing, but I don't know how else to explain it. Maybe after all our years together, some of her positive attitude and quest for happy endings finally rubbed off on me. I smiled, knowing that no matter what happened in the past, I loved my wife. With everything I was, I loved her. Nothing else mattered, and now a baby was involved. Somehow, I knew everything was going to be okay.

I was led to another waiting room outside of the operating room. I sat next to yet another set of white swinging doors.

I found myself wandering the halls of the hospital aimlessly, much as I had spent my life before I had met her—no direction or destination. I was walking up one corridor and down another. It was a never-ending maze of halls, all stark and white.

My pilgrimage came to an end when I found I was standing in front of the hospital chapel. The last time I went to church was for Tess's christening, which wasn't even my idea. Opening the door slowly, it was empty and perfectly silent. I walked in and headed straight to the altar. I went down on bended knees and started to pray. It came surprisingly easy for a fallen Catholic. All the emotions I had kept at bay my whole life now poured into my heart and my head as a broken dam spills its water. "Heavenly Father, I beg of you to spare my wife and the child she carries. They are both innocents. I promise to make it up to her. I will protect them and love them both. I will raise the child as my own. It is a part of her, and she is the best part of me. To take them would be the same as taking my soul. Dear God, if you can hear me, please answer my prayers."

I'm not sure how long I was in the chapel. Time was moving too slowly to calculate. I made my way back to the waiting room, where I found the surgeon looking for me. My heart sped up to the point where I thought I might have a heart attack.

I asked the only question that needed to be answered. "Is she okay?"

"We were able to release the pressure that had been building on her brain. So far, there does not appear to be any sign of neurological damage. However, it's still too early to tell conclusively. We will have a better idea in a couple of days."

A wave of relief washed over me, and then I realized he hadn't mentioned the baby. I was about to ask, but as I opened my mouth, the surgeon's beeper went off, and he left in a hurry. I would have to wait for an answer.

Chapter 41

HOURS LATER, A NURSE brought me into the recovery room, where I saw my beautiful bride in bed with tubes running into her thin arms, and her head bandaged tightly. She looked pale and frail. How was it possible that this was the same woman who sent up effervescent bubbles when she laughed and charmed a room with her child-like sense of humor? What had we done? What had I done?

I looked at the nurse who stood over her. "Can she hear me?"

"Talk to her. She will know you're here. I'm going to change her drip, and then I will leave you two alone."

I sat in the chair and held her hand. She didn't grip mine back. I kissed her cheek, and she didn't respond to that either. I spoke to her, telling her all the things I should have through the years.

"Hey baby, I'm here. Thank God you didn't leave me. You scared the shit out of me. You have to stay with me. Don't you know I can't live without you?

You saved me. You saved me from a dull, monotonous life. I always thought that I would end up alone. In fact, I was positive of it. I'm not sure how to tell you everything you mean to me and what you have done for me, but I'm going to try because I know how much it annoys you when I don't say anything.

God, I want to hear you laugh right now. I know you would have thought that was hilarious. You have the best laugh. I even think it's cute when you snort.

"When we met, I learned to appreciate things I had never given thought to before. You taught me to have fun and enjoy the simple things. Before you, I never noticed the colors in a sunrise. I was always too busy until you dragged my butt to the beach at five o'clock in the morning, more excited than a little girl on Christmas day. You taught me how to enjoy coffee and that it is more than just a hot drink.

"You are one of the goofiest and silliest women I have ever known, and I love it. I love how you sing off-key at the top of your lungs while you cook and dance with Tess and Jack in the kitchen. You have a way of lighting up our house, our home, filling it with energy and life. The children and I are so lucky to live a life filled with the goodness you bring to it.

"I'm going to tell you some secrets, but I'll deny them if you ever bring them up. I love to watch Real Housewives with you. I pretend I'm reading, but I'm really watching. Don't tell my brothers. I will never live it down!

"Here's a confession. When you have PMS, I purposely antagonize you. I figure you'll be all sensitive and mad, so I save up my aggravation all month and then let it fly. Sorry about that, but it is pretty funny.

"Jack and Tess miss you so much. You're such a fantastic mother. I am so proud of you. Sometimes I watch you with the children and wonder how you find the energy to keep up with them and how you always, always have enough love to go around. I love how you can simultaneously have a tea party with Tess and a lightsaber duel with Jack. Everyone is always saying what terrific kids we have, and it's all because of you, my love.

"Sometimes I sit outside Jack or Tess's room when you're in there, and I listen to you sing songs and say prayers with them at bedtime. Sometimes I get jealous of the love between you and the children. I want to be part of that. You have opened my eyes to a world I didn't know existed. Thank you for everything, my darling. You are my wife and my life, and I'm never going to let you go.

"Get some rest, baby. Get strong. I want you to come home. I'm going to stay here until you're ready to wake up. Don't worry about the children. Sarah is with them. I'm not going anywhere. I promise. You'll never be alone again." I put my head down next to her and fell asleep.

I woke hours later, her fingers gently smoothing my hair. I looked up to see her beautiful sparkling brown eyes looking back at me. "Are you okay?" I asked.

"Yeah," she said. "I was watching you sleep."

I smiled back at her. "Hey, you stole my line."

Chapter 42

AFTER THREE WEEKS, I was released from the hospital and returned home to Andrew, Jack, and Tess. The world had changed somehow.

I looked at the spot, still stained with my blood, and had to look away. How could I have done that? I swore I wouldn't be like her, but that is who I had become.

Instead of heading to the liquor cabinet or falling to my knees, I held the children's hands and asked everyone to sit with me.

"I am so sorry, everyone. I know it was scary when I was away. I was sick, which is why I fell. I am making a promise right here and now; nothing like that will ever happen again."

"Promise Mommy?" begged Tess.

"Cross my heart and hope to eat broccoli for the rest of my life."

"Ewww, that's gross." She pretended to gag.

"Why don't you monkeys go up and brush your teeth?"

As soon as they left the room, "Andrew, when I go put the children to bed, please throw out every bottle of booze and every ounce of liquor. I think I'm strong enough to handle it, but I cannot take any chances. I will not, I repeat, will not ever have them see me like that again." The lump in my throat grew to the size of a golf ball.

"Consider it done, my love." He didn't bat an eye.

By morning, it was all gone.

Although we are both healing, life is not the proverbial bed of roses. A lot of damage control still needs to be done, but we are both willing to do it.

As an individual, I need to make sure I never end up in that dark, ugly place again. It is time to take the demons out of hiding. I know I will never find peace until I do. I'm back to seeing Laura and learning a lot.

I don't think I will ever change entirely, nor do I want to. My scars run deep, but they have also helped me to become the person I am—the person who wants to help others. I want to learn how to cope better and become more centered. I don't want to be shaken to my very core every time I perceive I'm not being treated well. I need to extract the extremes. To do that, I have to accept how my childhood colored my life and how everything is interconnected.

I have always tried not to think of those times often, but I have to know. First, there is no denying being abused conditioned me to project my fears of being hurt, both physically and emotionally, onto the men in my life, not to mention how it affected my sense of self-worth. I have always been so sure someone was out to hurt me that I found a way to make it come true. Logically, I know what they did wasn't my fault, but I have spent my life being embarrassed and ashamed of who I am. I am still trying to convince myself I am not to blame, but changing a lifelong pattern is not easy. I'm hoping by identifying this part of me and bringing it to light, I will find a way to make peace with myself. The whole subject of childhood abuse is ugly, and no one wants to be a part of it. We all hope that if we ignore it, it will go away, but it won't.

If I look at this from an intellectual standpoint, I can see it is more than a statistic. It is an epidemic. It is the perpetrators who should run and hide, not the survivors.

Through all the soul searching I have been doing, I have found why I always have an intense need to help others. It's because no one helped me, and I don't want to let that happen to anyone else.

I have found the passion I was looking for two years ago. It is neither in art nor in the arms of another man. It is volunteering to help other victims of child abuse and neglect. As I continue the healing process, I hope I can give comfort to those who are struggling. I don't want anyone else to inflict pain on themselves that has no business there.

Next, we tackled my relationship with Jackie. Unfortunately, we recently found out Jackie is dying of pancreatic cancer. It's late-stage with no chance of recovery.

Laura didn't like to tiptoe around sensitive subjects. She was more of the rip-off the band-aid school of thought, "Do you love your mother?"

"Of course," I said without thinking about my answer. I think it had been my answer for so long it is practically a pre-programmed response. When I thought about it for more than thirty seconds, my answer was different. "Actually, I'm not sure. Sometimes I do, but to be brutally honest, sometimes I hate her so much I want to scream. Perhaps that's what I have been doing for so long. I've been screaming in my head and heart. I don't understand why she let everything happen and never helped me. What kind of mother ignores her children's safety for her own pleasure? Didn't she think I was worthy of her love and attention? Laura, I have a lot of questions and conflicting emotions as far as she is concerned. It's confusing to hate and love one person so much."

"That is completely normal, Julie. Let yourself experience the full range of emotions and then forgive yourself for feeling them. You need to give yourself a break. Allow the feelings that come to you and make them part of who you are. You don't have to feel bad for being human. You have every right to be angry. Actually, I'm surprised you have come through everything as well as you have."

"If this is coming through things well, I'd hate to see those who don't."

"Trust me, I have seen them, and you are doing remarkably well. You need to accept that you are not to blame for the world's problems and need to learn to look at things more objectively. Think a little more with your brain and less with your heart. It's going to take practice, but you can do it," she seemed very confident. I, however, was not at all sure.

I'm trying to remember what Laura said, and I think her advice is starting to work—I don't hate myself quite as much. Actually, I don't hate myself at all. Well, at least not so far this week. It is an awful lot of work trying to be normal.

Jackie is now in hospice. There was no way to keep her home anymore. I visit weekly, and I speak with her daily. We have talked about the past, but only in the broadest of terms. I am finding that deconstructing her psyche is not essential to my healing process. It is only in my best interest to accept her for who she is and forgive her for her mistakes. Jackie and I have spent our lives as mere acquaintances that have been forced by circumstance to be in each other's lives.

"Julie, I am so proud of you. You have turned into an intelligent, thought-provoking, and interesting person, my darling. How and when did you get so smart?" She asked with a smile during our last visit.

I was taken aback by her comment and confidently replied, "Through living life, Mom. It can teach us all sorts of things if we are open to listening and learning."

"It's obvious you have learned your lessons well. You are certainly more than just a pretty face." At hearing that, I was both relieved and angry. I was happy she finally realized I wasn't the stupid little girl she had always thought me to be, yet angry that I lived so much of my life believing her words to be true.

I took a deep breath and said, "I'm trying hard, Mom."

"You turned out to be a better woman than I," she paused and then said with a smile, "I want to be like you when I grow up."

I leaned over and hugged her. "Do you have any idea how long I have waited to hear something like that from you?"

"I'm sorry it took so long. I wish we had more time. I want to know you better. I've missed so much," her eyes welled with tears.

"Me too, but let's make the most of what we have left." I took a breath. "Hi, I'm Julie. So happy to meet you."

"I'm so happy to meet you too, Sweetheart. Julie, I'm not ready to go. I'm scared." Her voice was shaky as she held my hand as tightly as her weakened body would allow.

"I know, Mom. Don't be afraid. I will be here for you. I love you. You do know that, don't you?"

"Thanks, honey. I love you too. I'm a lucky woman."

"Yes, you are, Mom, and don't forget it." I smiled and winked at her. "I'm lucky too. I'll call you later." With that, I kissed her cheek.

After leaving the facility, I sat in my car and cried. Amazingly, we can finally accept we are two separate individuals, and we can respect our differences. As much as I have always prided myself on being so unlike her, I have discovered we are similar in many ways. We are both dramatic, great storytellers, often highly emotional, and frequently over the top. We are smart, sexy, and at times, extremely silly.

We are also both self-destructive alcoholics with a penchant for hiding where it is dark.

I understand that I can become untethered, just like her, if I am not very careful. Some of the same traits that embarrassed me most as a child are some of the same qualities I find undeniable in myself. Isn't it ironic how that happens? I think—I hope I have broken the cycle.

The following Sunday, my phone rang at dawn. It was the nursing home, letting me know that Mom had passed away. They said she fell asleep and didn't wake up. There was no more pain in her body or soul.

"Ms. Julie, your mom talked about you all the time. She told everyone who would listen how smart her Julie was, and her grandchildren, who were so brilliant that they would win the Nobel Prize. She told me one of the little ones has her hands. Do you know what that means?"

"I do," I said, smiling through the tears. "My daughter Tess has long, beautiful fingers, just like her grandma."

"Well, she loved you all very much. The front desk will be in touch. My deepest condolences."

"Thank you."

Andrew held me as I wept. It was over. I wanted her to die for so long, and now she was finally gone. Was it wrong to feel relieved?

Chapter 43

Of course, Laura and I are discussing my relationship with Andrew at great lengths. I want to see the good in my husband, not the bad; he is kind and decent. We just happened to have some terrible stuff happen. Probably not unlike most other people. A part of me never stopped loving him. He is not perfect, but neither am I. I was angry. Sometimes I still am. I have spent so much time blaming him for the domino effect of events that I was blind to and no longer saw who he was. In my eyes, he became another man trying to ruin me. I didn't remember all the wonderful traits I had fallen in love with so long ago. I may not have started our downward spiral, but I did my fair share of damage as we were sinking.

We are now in couple's therapy. I am spending my mornings with Laura and afternoons with Patty, our therapist, and Andrew. Half my days are spent sitting on a couch, talking to doctors. I do have to admit I love therapy for purely narcissistic reasons. I am paying someone to listen to me talk about whatever I want for as long as I want, and I don't have to feel guilty about monopolizing the conversation. I kept everything in for so long, never daring to tell the whole story, and now no one can shut me up. I have learned the hard way; if I don't deal with the issues as they arise, they will find a way to rear their ugly head, and probably not in the healthiest ways.

Marriage is a hell of a lot of work. I'm not sure if it's this hard for everyone, but it certainly has been for us. We are working tirelessly to make sure the lessons we have learned from this experience take hold. It would be far too easy for us to backslide into previous patterns, and neither of us wants to ever go there again.

Patty has had us engage in various exercises to help us remember why we fell in love in the first place. We started by revisiting our past. It seems we have both forgotten the fun times. Once we started, it was pretty easy.

"Julie, why don't you go first? Tell me something funny or loving about Andrew."

"Hmm." I thought out loud.

"Is it so hard, Jul?" Andrew's mouth turned down.

"Yeah, it is. Sorry." My lips twisted in annoyance.

"Take your time." Patty continued to lead us calmly.

"Okay, I have it. When we first bought our house, we didn't have any money to hire people to fix it up, so we did it ourselves. One night around eleven, we were both punch drunk and got into a paint fight." I started to laugh.

"Oh yeah. Your hair was zebra-striped for a week." Andrew said, joining our trip down memory lane.

We both laughed at the pictures dancing in our heads. What we didn't say out loud was that we made love on the kitchen floor, and the paints on our bodies swirled together, creating a mosaic of color.

"Your turn, Andrew," Patty prompted.

"Let me see."

"It's not so easy when you're put on the spot, is it?" I jabbed at him.

"No, it is. I just have to decide which one." He drummed his fingers upon his cheek. "When we were dating, we went to the Catskill Mountains for a hike."

"I remember. We got lost. How was that funny?" I asked.

"Patty said funny or loving. This is both. Jul and I decided to go for a hike on a glorious autumn day to see the leaves change. We took a walk along a well-marked path. Well, it was well-marked for those who paid attention. We didn't understand how it happened, but we got lost. It took us five hours to work our way back. The sun was almost gone, and it was turning cold. During those five hours, we wandered around aimlessly. We witnessed some incredible sights. Beautiful waterfalls were flowing into deep, pristine lakes, leaves redder than fire, and baby wolves nursing from their mother. Remember when we talked about if we couldn't find our way out?" His lips curled up in a subtle smile.

"Yes. You said if we were going to die, at least we would be together."

"I still feel that way." He took my hand in his.

"Thank you. I need to hear things like that," I began to soften.

"I'm going to try to say it more often. I love you. I really love you, Julie," His eyes were glossy with emotion.

Although the strongest memories have been the ones from when everything went wrong, there are so many good ones tucked away in a holding cell somewhere. We only need to discover them again.

Patty has also pointed out that somewhere along the line, we stopped listening. We didn't hear what was being said between the lines. We each have emotional baggage. Our sensitivities echo somewhere in our past, and the people we love need to be aware of them. We are both at fault.

Andrew requires help to express himself. It is not something that comes naturally to him. He was told to "shut up and be a man" for so long that he doesn't understand his feelings or how to express them. He needs to be reminded he is not alone and that we are all in this together. He doesn't need to be perfect. I love him for his faults as well as his finer qualities. I will be patient and his guide, as long as he remains fully invested in us.

He needs to remember that I am more than what I seem. I am not the invincible go-getter the outside world sees. My soul is tender and needs to be nurtured. I am scared all the time. Although the exterior wounds healed long ago, my invisible scars will always remain. I need to learn how to trust, and he will help me navigate this unfamiliar territory.

Lastly, we need to fall in love again, and I think we are on our way. When he walks in the door at night,

I'm happy he's home and kiss him tenderly. He has started to give me compliments again.

"Hi everyone. I'm home!" Andrew yells as he walks in the door.

"Daddy! Daddy!" The children go running towards him.

"Hey, how are my kiddos?"

"Good, Daddy."

"Where's your mommy?"

"In there." Jack points to the kitchen.

As I removed the lasagna from the oven, his arms slipped around my waist.

"Hey, watch out! I don't want to burn you," I scold him.

"I can't help myself. You and lasagna, it doesn't get any better than that!"

He backs off, and I put down the scorching hot pan and watch him as he picks up Tess.

"How's my little princess?" I remember hearing my father say those very same words to Sarah. I'm happy Tess has a father who loves her.

Jack comes into the kitchen, and we slow dance. All four of us, singing loudly and off-key.

We are laughing a lot these days. Not only do Andrew and I sleep in the same room or the same bed, but we sleep in each other's arms where we can feel the other's heartbeat.

A funny thing happened last week. Andrew was officially informed he needs reading glasses. I went to Macy's with Jack and Tess in tow to buy him his first pair. As I held the black frames up to my face to see how they would look on me, I realized that we would be one of those couples at a restaurant, taking turns with the reading glasses while looking at the menu. Oddly, I find the image exceptionally romantic. We truly are growing old together, just as we had promised to do more than ten years ago.

Chapter 44

LAST NIGHT, WHILE I was sitting in bed, Andrew walked in holding two ice cream sundaes. "Anyone order Chocolate Moose Tracks with hot fudge sauce, lots of whipped cream, and chocolate sprinkles?"

"I believe that would be mine. Thank you, kind sir." I nodded my head to him.

"You're welcome, Madam. May I join you?"

"It would be my pleasure," I giggled and patted the bed next to me.

When we finished, I contently leaned back in his arms. They are strong, comforting, and his touch is warm on my skin. Tears began to trickle down my face. This time, not in pain or anger, but in gratitude. Gratitude that we have been given a chance to rebuild our lives and our love.

I took Andrew's hand and placed it on my stomach. "Uh oh, we're going to need a bigger freezer. It looks like we have another ice cream lover here." Andrew laughed. "Wow, it's strong!"

"Yup, a real fighter." I rubbed my belly to settle the little imp down.

"Just like its mommy," and he kissed me gently.

We both acknowledged that in a few short months, our family would grow. We would be adding one colicky, non-sleeping, but beautiful baby. Despite biology, this child is ours. The living miracle inside me would not be a reminder of everything we have done wrong. Instead, it will be a testament to everything we are doing right.

"I love you, Mr. Russo," I said with a smile.

"I love you too, Mrs. Russo."

"I can't believe we made it."

"I never had a doubt." He held my hand, kissing my palm. "I was never going to let you go."

Chapter 45

IT'S FALL AGAIN. THE leaves are burning with color, and the cool air is beginning to make an appearance. The changes over the last year seem almost as if they were a dream. I am constantly amazed by what life has in store for me.

I'm looking forward to wearing sweaters and taking the children apple picking.

While walking into town to have lunch, Jack debates his sister on the local diner's culinary expertise. "Mommy, they have the best chicken fingers!"

"No way, Jose. Their hot dogs are the best!" Tess needles him.

"Yes, way!" Jack yells.

They continued to argue as we crossed the street. Jack, Tess, and I hold hands as Andrew pushes baby Lilly in the stroller.

"Are you two going to fight the whole time?" I ask.

"Sorry, Mom, but she is sooo annoying!" Jack sneers.

"Am not!"

"Are too!"

Once on the other side, we all notice, as usual, a wedding was about to take place at the big white church.

"Mommy, can we watch the pretty wedding girls?" begged Tess.

"Sure, honey. See the girl in the white dress? She's the one who is going to get married, and the other ones are her friends."

"Oh, they are so pretty," she says, clasping her hands together in wonder.

Watching the bride took me back to the day that changed my life. She turned around, and we locked gazes for a moment and smiled. She looked at Andrew, the children, and back at me. "I hope someday I'll be that lucky," she called out.

I replied in all sincerity, "I hope you are too."

It has been months since we began our work with Laura and Patty, and I'm sure we have a lot more ahead of us, but for the first time in as long as I can remember, I am sleeping through the night. I'm not having nightmares, and I am doing it without drugs of any kind. I no longer hear screams in the darkness or have faceless people chasing me and pinning me to the ground. This journey has been long and trying on my soul, but my heart feels whole again. I think I finally found that home I longed for as a little girl. I realize it was never a place. It was a feeling.

I am home. I am loved. I am a survivor.

If you enjoyed this story, please consider leaving a review on Amazon and/or Goodreads. Writing a book is a labor of love, and authors are always grateful for feedback from their readers.

a amazon.com/Vikki-Alexander/e/B08YXQ78XC/ref =aufs_dp_fta_dsk

g goodreads.com/author/show/21259921.Vikki_Alex ander

O instagram.com/author_vikki_alexander/

Acknowledgments

Writing this novel has been a labor of love. What started as a mid-life crisis-driven project turned into a mission to help others as well as entertain. There are many human experiences the general population keeps buried under a shroud of secrecy. They are the very topics that need exploration. They need a voice.

Thank you to all the women who have shared their stories. These pioneers are paving the way for future generations of women to have a voice greater than our own.

Thank you to my husband, who has never doubted my ability to succeed in anything I take on. I know I am a handful, and I appreciate you giving me the time and space I needed to make Coloring Life a reality.

Thank you to my children, who are my light and my life. Thank you for letting me drone on endlessly about new ideas, titles, and book covers. Most of all, thank you for being two of the most amazing humans I know. I am proud of you every day. I am so blessed to be your mother.

A special shout out to Grace, my daughter, who talked me into taking this old manuscript out of my closet and publishing it. I believe her words were, "Mom, you always tell us to do something we love. It's time you take your own advice." If it wasn't for her, this would never have seen the light of day. Thank you, Maye.

Thank you, Gina Randall, for my lessons in novel writing 101. I am still lost but finding my way, thanks to you.

Thank you, Cindy Shelton, my first and most enthusiastic beta reader. I will never forget the day you finished the first draft and begged me to write another book. Your support means more to me than I can ever express.

Thank you, Dr. Lisa Cappalletti, for spending hours with me discussing the human condition. Who knew when we started delving into the complexities of humanity at seventeen, we would continue it into adulthood.

Thank you, Daina Gonzalez, for being the keeper of all my secrets. You have always been my touchstone.

Thank you, Marla Daniels, my structural editor, for delicately and professionally showing me the error of my ways, and there were a lot of them.

Thank you, Tiffany Persaud, of Burden of Proofreading, for coming to my rescue. Your kindness and keen eye saved my sanity.

Thank you to all who read the variations of Coloring Life throughout the editing process. I am incredibly grateful for your time, support, and feedback.

Last but not least, thank you to my Tenafly Chicks. You ladies 'fill my heart.'

All our dreams can come true if we have the courage to pursue them.
- Walt Disney

About Author

Vikki Alexander is a lifelong New Jersey resident. When she isn't creating fictional characters contending with real-world issues, she can be found hiking, exploring waterfalls, or hanging out with her family.

If you enjoyed Julie's story in Coloring Life, be sure to pick The Many Loves of Sarah Brennan, where you will get to know Julie's sister.

a amazon.com/Vikki-Alexander/e/B08YXQ78XC/ref =aufs_dp_fta_dsk

g goodreads.com/author/show/21259921.Vikki_Alexander

instagram.com/author_vikki_alexander/

Also By

The Many Loves of Sarah Brennan
Coming of age in the 1980s wasn't easy, especially as the eldest daughter of an alcoholic divorcee and an absentee father. Sarah and her sister Julie are constantly fighting ghosts that haunt their relationships and lives.
When Sarah falls in love with the handsome new stranger, everything she has been brought up to believe comes into question.

A tragic accident rips Sarah's world apart, sending her in search of inner peace and purpose. Her travels take her from the suburban streets of New Jersey to the tranquility of Sedona, the turquoise water of Crete, and the towering steel skyscrapers of Manhattan.

Will Sarah overcome her past or let it ruin her chance at happiness?

a amazon.com/Vikki-Alexander/e/B08YXQ78XC/ref =aufs_dp_fta_dsk

g goodreads.com/author/show/21259921.Vikki_Alex ander

instagram.com/author_vikki_alexander/